Perspective

PERSPECTIVE

How the Power of a Biblical Perspective can Change your Life

Charity Ritter

ISBN: 978-1-936286-00-3

Please go to the Bible for context to Scriptures referenced.

Published by Discovery Gadget LLC
DiscoveryGadget.com

 DISCOVERY
GADGET

TABLE OF CONTENTS

INTRODUCTION

Dear Friend, Here is my heart.

Throughout my life, I have struggled with many things. At times, life has been significantly tough on me. I share this not to complain—many have endured much worse than I have—rather I share this because the ups and downs of life have contributed to the stress and anxiety I've endured. More importantly, sharing this is a great testament to what I've survived.

This book will outline many of those tough times. I've endured and ultimately survived the loops on the rollercoaster of my life.

I used to be a constant ball of stress and anxiety; I was someone who worried about many things. My brain would shoot adrenaline through my body at the smallest of upsets often leaving me tense, sleep-deprived, in pain, angry, and highly stressed. Even my son, only four years old at the time, would pray for me not to be stressed because he could feel my stress affecting him.

While I still experience the ups and downs of life, I am now better able to endure life's twists and turns without my entire nervous system sinking into the gutter. I am now better able to handle the rollercoaster of life without unleashing a fountain of fury onto my loved ones. I am now able to look at myself in the mirror and see what God sees rather than seeing the many flaws that the world has insisted I see. It has been a long journey, and I still have a long road ahead as I continue to grow.

What has made the most significant impact on me is that I found power in my perspective. This one small shift has developed in me greater strength and happiness while decreasing my stress. Simply put, developing a perspective that is based on biblical truth has changed my life. It has changed me. It has transformed my soul. Not only has it changed the way I think, but most important-ly, it has transformed my entire life by encountering the healing power of Jesus Christ. Through an ever-deepening relationship with God I was able to change the way I thought about things and my circumstances. In turn, I have discovered freedom from stress, anxiety, and fear. I have grown in love and grace for others.

Maybe you have never given much thought to whether or not there is a God, or maybe you know that there's something out there but think that what that is cannot be determined. Maybe you have known God all your life, or maybe you're just starting to meet with Him. Regardless of where you are in relation to God, I want to start with this truth: There is a God. Jesus Christ is God, and He reconciled believers back to Him by paying for it with His life. He loves you more than you could ever understand, and He desires for you to love Him back. If you have picked up this book, I believe that He—Jesus—is calling you to a deeper relationship with Him.

Friend, I encourage you to read through these chapters with the intention of reflecting on your own life that you might grow in your relationship with Jesus. As you draw closer to Jesus, your life will be changed forever. You will find a purpose and a fulfillment that you have never known before. This book is my story of how

Jesus has changed my life and how He can change yours too.

I grew up knowing Jesus as my Savior but like a lot of Christians, I have spent years making my faith personal. After many trials and struggles, I am not shy to now say, "I love Jesus, and I long for my life to be a witness to His ever-reaching power and love for us as believers." I'm married with three wonderful kids. I'm also a licensed therapist, business owner, and now a Christian author. I am not a theologian or a preacher, but I am passionate about God's truths and how they can be applied to our lives. I believe that God uses His Word—the words He gives us through the Bible—to teach us personally within the context of our lives, and I will use God's Word in this book, along with illustrations from my own life experiences, to explain how I apply God's Word to my life. Rather than focusing on the details of nuanced theological concepts, I will focus largely on how the Bible offers us a healthier perspective on life.

Though I am a therapist and some of the content of this book comes from my profession, I write this book primarily from a Christian author's perspective. Most of the truths in this book have emerged from my own personal sanctification process, although other personal and professional experiences such as my role as a therapist, business owner, and parent, are woven in as well.

For those of you who love Jesus and have surrendered your lives to Him, the Holy Spirit lives inside of you. The Bible tells us that the Holy Spirit brings the words of God to life in our hearts. Everyday God uses biblical principles to help me with my perspectives. For instance, I might be in a certain situation in which I feel a tug on my heart from the Holy Spirit. That simple and quiet interception from the Holy Spirit then reminds me of a biblical passage that in turn helps me to understand, interpret, or change my perspective on that situation. Maybe you can relate to that experience or maybe you cannot. Regardless, the Holy Spirit works in the lives of Christians in often subtle ways.

We are all so different, and we all have different ways of understanding, processing, and applying information. Some are more creative, while others are more logical. The awesome thing is that our Creator, who knows every strand of hair on our heads (including the ones that are turning gray), knows exactly how we need Him to personally guide us and intimately comfort us. If my sanctification process differs from your experience, that's normal. You might even go so far as to say it's expected.

In my twenties, I worked with a lady who seemed to have this figured out. You could tell by the way she talked about her life that she was using a biblical and eternal lens to filter how she thought about things. Though I only knew her for a short time, her Christlike perspective on life was evident. She exuded peace in the midst of stressful situations, and her view of others was filled with a love and grace that could only come from Jesus. I remember praying to God, asking Him to grow me and allow me to be more like her. At the time, she had grown children, and she was probably in her sixties, so I still have some time. However, sometimes I feel so far from where I want to be.

There are times when God shows me something that is wrong with the way that I am thinking. In that moment, my heart experiences such a sense of clarity that it makes me excited to know that God is intimately leading me. I actually feel a burden lifted from my shoulders that I didn't even realize was there. In those moments, the Holy Spirit helps me to correct my thinking. He brings me to a place where I can see His hand at work in my life and how He is growing me in my perspective. Then I return to my day-to-day life with kids, work and chores, and it's often like I forgot what my heart knew so clearly only a few minutes ago. Sometimes I go right back to wrong thinking patterns and faulty thinking as if I completely forgot how God had grown me previously.

I have wondered if there is something wrong with my memory at times. Maybe I'm eating the wrong foods, not getting enough sleep, or maybe it's something else, like ADHD. I used to think that maybe it was just a mom thing. Maybe it was all those estrogen hormones that saturated my brain for nine-plus months multiplied by three pregnancies. But as I talk to others, I am learning that I am not alone. It's actually pretty normal to forget like that. Since it is not specific to me, maybe this issue of forgetfulness is universal to all of us.

That is why I wrote this book. Every time that God taught me something that lifted my spirit or eased a burden by straightening my distorted perspective, I wrote it down. At first, I started blogging these teachable moments but the lessons continued to expand and multiply. Eventually I had enough recorded to fill a book, and so I did just that. I wrote this book for me (for my brain to remember) and for you. I have always felt called to help others, and I hope this book helps you.

This book is my love story. It is a love story between myself and my Creator, and it details the trials, hardships, adventures, and successes I needed to experience in order to embrace the depth of my Creator's love and purpose for me. I wrote it so that I can look back and read through it again and again and remember the lessons that God has taught me over the years. I don't want to keep fighting the same battles. Satan wants us fighting the same battles over and over so that we are stuck rather than moving forward.

I wrote this book to help me keep my thoughts on biblical and eternal things, and it is my prayer that maybe these lessons can help you as well. Use the companion workbook to allow yourself to work through these issues in your life, and keep it handy so you can look back and remember the changes God will make in your life through this process. Your life will change as you apply a Christ-centered perspective to the trials, hardships, adventures, and successes in your life from the past and in the future.

Friend, In order to break the cycle of fighting the same battles over and over again, we have to first understand why having a proper perspective is such a powerful component of the battle that we are fighting. Once we better understand the power of our perspective, we can then begin to develop a proper mindset on key concepts in our situations. Then we can start applying a proper perspective in our lives, ultimately impacting our understanding of God, Satan, our identity, our purpose, our everyday life, and our calling.

CHAPTER 1

THE POWER OF YOUR PERSPECTIVE

Although we rarely have the power to change our circumstances, we do have the ability to change our perspective—how we think and assign meaning to our circumstances. Our perspective on a situation has power. It has the power to keep us stuck in defeat or to get us through tough times. The way we look at life can ruin blessings, or it can turn trials and suffering into opportunities. Even when our circumstances are as overwhelming as a diagnosable mental illness, I have found in counseling sessions that a simple change in perspective has the power to turn things around for my clients.

Through my experiences with my own counseling, Christian training, and mentorship, and also through my career as a therapist and business owner, I have encountered both false perspectives in myself as well as in other people. We live in a culture that tells us we can believe in whatever we want and claim it as our truth. The world wants to define us with a variable truth ruled by our fickle emotions. However, as followers of Christ, the Bible teaches us that there is an absolute truth—something that is true in every circumstance and cannot be changed.

All of us have some kind of inaccurate perspective that would benefit from being better aligned with a biblical and eternal reality. We have interpreted our experiences through the lens and meaning that the world ingrained in us rather than seeing our experiences through the lens and meaning that the Bible offers us.

We all have times when our mindset hinders us and affects our lives significantly. These untrue definitions of what we understand our thoughts and experiences to mean can attempt to hinder and sabotage the good work God is doing in our lives. Sometimes we don't even realize it because there is so much depth in how our skewed perspective has developed over time. In these instances, the only answer seems to be "well whatever seems true to you must be fine."

Even as Christians, we are sometimes enticed toward this way of thinking. When we try to offer comfort or Scripture to someone in pain, and it doesn't always deliver the emotional results we hoped it would, it is easy to give up and agree that maybe things won't change. Sometimes God shows us His truth in a moment and we change our perspective almost instantly, whereas other times the depth of our false perspectives prevent us from receiving what God has for us. It is in those instances that our thoughts, definitions and perspectives need to be unraveled and identified in order for them to be aligned with a Christlike perspective. Either way, changing your mindset is not a quick-fix. Even when it seems to be quick, we still have to hold onto that new understanding for it to truly change us.

What is Perspective?

Perspective is your understanding or definition of reality. It is your mindset on how things should be in life. It is the meaning that you have assigned to your experiences and your circumstances. It is the lens through which you experience the world according to your own logic, your past experiences, and your unique understandings. Everything that you think and feel is filtered through the lens of your perspective.

Perspective starts with the thoughts that we have about something and what we believe those thoughts mean about us, others, and the world around us. Those thoughts then develop the framework of our understanding and how we respond to things out of that understanding. Our thoughts and our perspectives are connected. The two work together. Having a positive and true perspective and thought process can make the difference between success and failure. A biblical perspective can allow you to respond to a situation with patience, maturity, and peace rather than responding purely out of emotions that likely stem from an unhealthy meaning you previously assigned to that situation.

Recently my husband and I started a new hobby. We have been bouldering, which is a short version of wall climbing. In bouldering, the climber does not use ropes and does not climb extremely high. However, in bouldering, the problems that the climber faces are complex. As the climber moves to the top of the wall, he or she must travel up, over, sideways, and even upside down. Though it is a bit dangerous, and though I did suffer one fall that sent me to a chiropractor, bouldering is a great workout, a great way to challenge your problem-solving skills, and a wonderful practice in positive self-talk.

In the short time I have been bouldering, I have seen the difference my perspective makes in achieving a successful climb. If I am halfway up the wall and the problem is increasingly challeng-ing, my arms will start to tire, making the next hand grip seem just out of reach. This is when my self-talk can make all the difference. If I can tell myself, "You are strong," "You've got this," "You are athletic" and "You might be able to make it." I can usually hold on just a little longer allowing me to reach a grip that I otherwise perceived out of reach. But if I say to myself, "Shoot, I am getting tired," "I don't know if I can do this," or "It's too far," I almost cer-tainly will either fall off the wall or be forced to climb down. When my thoughts are positive, I can push myself harder and make it to the finish more often. The power of perspective in bouldering makes the difference between success and failure, and the same is true for life.

What if your perspective isn't where it should be?

What if your perceived reality is inaccurate?

Our culture tell us that truth is all relative anyway, and that what is true for me might not be true for you. But if you are a follower of Jesus Christ, then the Bible tells us something totally different.

According to Scripture, there is an absolute truth and a right way to think. Your perspective will have a significant impact on your thoughts, feelings, stress levels, and relationships. We also put the intentions and motives of others through the same lens of perceived reality. If you are a follower of Christ, the Bible is clear about our perspective; it is to be Christ-centered.

An entire secular theoretical model of psychotherapy, Cog-nitive Behavioral Therapy, or CBT, is based on this same reality about our perspectives. CBT uses terms such as *schemas* and *core beliefs*, but these are the same concepts as perspectives. I, however, will approach this concept from a more biblical perspective, so we will not focus on CBT terms.

My early career in clinical counseling was limited to a traditional focus. Since working in private practice, I have had some clients with whom I was able, at their request, to use a biblical perspective alongside a clinical perspective. When a Christlike perspective is used in the counseling session, the level of healing and freedom the client experiences far outweighs those whose treatment is only taken from a clinical scope. Without a biblical perspective, where does one draw purpose, direction, or meaning for their life? Many people who experience mental illness would say that the largest symptoms of their illness stem from a lack of joy. Real joy comes from understanding our purpose. There is power in your perspective.

Intrusive Thoughts

An interesting example about the power of perspective comes from a counseling concept known as *intrusive thoughts*. Intrusive thoughts are one of the main symptoms of diagnosable anxiety disorders. Intrusive thoughts are quick and passing negative thoughts that cause one to be distressed or disturbed, and they can include angry thoughts, inappropriate or sexual thoughts, doubting relationships, negative self-talk, or many other things. Oftentimes people who are overly analytical or prone to anxiety assign meaning to those thoughts, and they allow those meanings to define who they believe themselves to be.

In other words, many of us have negative or unusual passing thoughts, but the danger is when we take that passing thought, dwell on it, assign meaning to it, and translate it into something we believe about who we are. When we do this, a passing thought turns into a lingering thought, and a lingering thought starts to cause us to question our identity and perspective on life.

Those who are susceptible to this danger are often disproportionately focused on those angry, inappropriate, or distressing thoughts. In treatment of these intrusive thoughts, one of the biggest remedies is to help the client understand that these thoughts are meaningless and should not define them. Secular psychology explains that intrusive thoughts are random brain firings, and they are not a window into an individual's internal self or subconsciousness. In fact, intrusive thoughts often reveal something that is out of alignment with a person's internal self, which contributes to the stress and anxiety one experiences when those uninvited thoughts emerge.

Both Christian psychologists and secular counseling models would agree that these thoughts come into the mind without placing any "fault" on the person for having the thoughts. They also agree that these thoughts will trigger emotions within us if we do not either quickly dismiss them or if we analyze them against a more positive truth. In Christian counseling, that truth is the Truth of Scripture.

So, the same culture that tells us we should do what feels right simultaneously acknowledges that our thoughts do not always mean what we think they do. Someone might have thoughts of hurting another person out of anger when in fact the one who is suffering the intrusive thoughts is actually a very kind and loving individual who would never want to harm another person.

One psychology model explains that these anxious thoughts are happening because the character of a kind and loving person finds thoughts of hurting someone to be so immensely distressing. The likelihood of that person acting on such thoughts is rather low. *(Be advised, if someone you know is having thoughts of hurting themselves or others, they need to be assessed by a professional therapist or psychologist. If these thoughts are not simply passing intrusive anxious thoughts, the person could act on them. This situation does need to be taken seriously for their safety.)*

There are some thoughts that are just meaningless and are passing intrusive thoughts. However, when we allow intrusive thoughts to carry too much weight in our lives, we risk becoming confused about who we are at our core. A loving and kind person who gives power to a passing thought of hurting another person may actually begin to believe that he/she is violent. In turn, that intrusive thought is fueled and begins to grow bigger. This is how nurturing an unwanted intrusive thought can lead to damaging one's perception of self. Secular psychology makes it clear, intrusive thoughts are meaningless and should be ignored. They are not worthy of a reaction or analysis, and most certainly they do not define a person.

When we analyze this concept further, we begin to understand the potential power of our intrusive thoughts and the danger of believing they have meaning. If the random negative thoughts you have about your marriage actually stem from intrusive thoughts, then maybe you are in a mostly happy marriage. If the doubts you have about making a big decision are intrusive thoughts then maybe you are actually making the right choice and consequently you can experience peace about the decision rather than anxiety. If the thoughts you have about your boss are intrusive thoughts, then you likely don't hate your job like you have allowed yourself to think. If the inappropriate sexual thoughts that are causing you to spiral into a pit of confusion are actually intrusive thoughts, then you don't need to obsessively doubt your sexuality, gender, or intimate relationships. Rather, you can rest in trusting that God made you just the way you are. He did not make a mistake.

Your perspective makes a difference. The way you think about things, especially the way you think about your passing thoughts, makes a difference.

What if you adopted the perspective that many of the passing thoughts that enter your mind might mean nothing? Would you avoid overanalyzing your feelings? Would you stop assigning negative meaning to every passing thought?

From a Christian counseling understanding, it seems clear to me that sometimes those intrusive thoughts could also actually be lies. What if those lies in our intrusive thoughts are part of Satan's strategy to trip us up?

Assuming that is true, then those intrusive lies have absolutely no validity in defining who we are because they may not even be coming from within us, but rather from outside of us. They could actually be part of the war that Satan has waged on our souls. It may be Satan trying to tempt us into something that our heart doesn't even want. It could be that the temptation is to obsess over the thoughts, or it could be to follow through on what the thoughts are about. Satan comes to steal and destroy (John 10:10). Intrusive thoughts that bring about shame, uncertainty, condemnation, and anxiety to a follower of Christ are not from God. The Bible warns about temptation. When we hold onto those intrusive thoughts and when we allow them to define us, we sabotage much of the peace, joy, and hope that God has promised for our lives.

Power of Perspective in Defining Who We Are

The average person can tell you their name, where they live, and the title of their job. Those are the objective variables about our identity. We often think those things answer the question, "Who are you?" However, when it comes to understanding a person's inner-self, personality-quirks, desires, motivations, purpose, and heart, answering the question, *Who are you?*, is not so easy.

The subjective variables of our identity are largely social constructs. The way in which we define ourselves has to do with the relationships we have, what we see other people doing, and what appears to be acceptable in our culture. For many of us, we misunderstand who we are because we are defining ourselves based on the wrong variables, human ideals, and secular culture, instead of biblical truth. For many years I struggled with defining myself using the wrong variables.

Until recently, I believed that there was something wrong with my personality. I was always much different from others. I was more serious, goal-focused, and blunt than most people. While I cared about people very much, and while I tried to do what I could to make others happy in a task-oriented way, I am not a people-pleaser in a relational sense. When I try to be more relational, I am unsuccessful. I present myself with confidence even when I do not feel confident, and I have always been an independent person. I wear my emotions right on my face, and if I am stressed most people can see it. I am extraverted when working on some things, especially if I am passionate about them, but I am introverted in social interactions. This sometimes translates to others that I am unfriendly, uncaring, and unapproachable. I have always wished people could see past how they interpreted my actions, and into my heart. Once people get to know me, they better understand my heart. However, growing up with this personality left me with a feeling that I should just stay away from people because they will never understand me. Many times I even believed that there was something defective with how God made me because I believed the negative feedback that I received from others about how they defined who I was.

As a child, others viewed me as bossy, mean, and a know-it-all. For many years this was how I defined myself. As a teenager, my peers often saw me as a threat, assuming that I thought I was better than others. Some labeled me as not fun, and for a few years this was how I defined myself. As an adult, I am still sometimes seen by some as uncaring and too serious. Sometimes I am tempted to define myself this way because if others see me that way, then it seems to be true. Even though I know that those things are not true about me, when many different people have defined me the same way for years and years, it is easy to think that I am a terrible person who is unable to relate to others.

Throughout my life, there were times that I would cry out to God asking why He made me this way. The rejection I felt from people for whom I cared deeply made me want to hide from everyone. Some years I hated myself, some years I was annoyed with everyone else. And some years I was frustrated at who God made me to be. When I was young, I wished I was someone else. Even though I am not a people-pleaser, I still defined who I was based on how other people saw me, and it made me miserable. Every time that I made someone feel like I did not care about them, my heart broke and I wished I could relate more easily to others.

I carried this perspective about myself at a core level, and it hurt every time another person experienced me as unfriendly or uncaring. I never understood why no one saw me for me, and why no one could see my heart. I care deeply for others, holding a deep value for people, and I never understood how others didn't see that in me. It made me feel invisible.

Although many may not realize this about me, and even though I am not a people pleaser, I am willing and often try to sacrifice my own needs, desires and preferences to meet the needs of others. I put so much effort toward being nice, smiling, and inquiring of others, that I am often left exhausted. It requires that I push myself out of my comfort zone to make sure people know that I care about them. I do this because I do love and care for people. I want others to feel supported by me, but the ways in which my love and care are best communicated to others does not come naturally to me.

Even though I hoped I would grow out of the miscommunication people perceive about my heart, the same misunderstandings have continued to arise into my adulthood. Over time I have learned that when the stress of life increases above what is normal, I lack the energy to push myself out of my comfort zone. I then default to my natural personality style, the same one that causes people to have a negative experience when they interact with me.

As I spent time with Jesus, it became clear to me that I had been defining myself with the wrong variables. I had either lost my focus on God, or I never really embraced how God defined me. Now that I have this insight and awareness, I am more intentional when I interact with others, paying attention to my actions and behaviors when I am under stress. Through a Christlike perspective, God has helped me to see that sometimes others are looking to me for personal validation. If others perceive me as uncaring, it very well might be because they are not receiving what they hoped as a result of their own insecurities. Becoming aware of this has helped me to develop a tool that I can use during those stressful and exhausting seasons.

I have found that it is easy enough to simply apologize for making others feel a certain way. In those times, I hold onto compassion for their struggle rather than exerting tremendous personal effort to ensure that I am being well received, which often results in my heart growing bitter. It's easier to say "I'm sorry" and try to smile at people than it is to try and explain my unique personality style to everyone. Although I do still try to initiate small talk and be more encouraging, I have stopped defining myself based on how people do or do not understand me.

My husband helped me see this new perspective. He thought back to when we first met and analyzed how I made him feel. He helped me to see that this misunderstanding was not about me, rather it was about how my confidence and independence can make others feel negatively about themselves. If others think I feel negatively about them due to lack of pleasantries, then that feels like evidence for them to define themselves negatively too. Perhaps the way people were experiencing me or perceiving me had more to do with them than it had to do with me. However, because relational niceties are a bit more challenging for me, I do try to improve this so that others know their value when they interact with me.

Redefining myself and better understanding what was happening in these situations allowed me to change my perspective about myself. No longer do I need to question God about why

He made me the way that He did. I am proud to be independent, confident, and different from others. Now that I am able to define myself as God defines me, I can practice offering encouragement to others rather than hiding and writing-off people all together. In relating to others, I can rely on the tools I am learning rather than assume that something is wrong with me. It also has helped me to look back and reframe my entire life, allowing me to experience healing from past broken relationships and rejection. That is the power of a biblical perspective in defining ourselves.

Without Proper Perspective

A proper perspective is something that has to be learned; it does not come naturally. Our perspectives begin taking shape as early as our first memories. I remember an interaction with my oldest son when he was young that helped me to better understand how God invites us to use His Word to change our perspectives. My son was learning a lesson that is difficult for each of us at some time or another. He was learning how to be patient and grateful. While playing with his toys, he felt the urge to use the bathroom. Instead of simply going into the bathroom, using the toilet, and returning to play, he made a detour into the kitchen where I was standing. He was visibly upset, and he started yelling, "Why do I always have to go to the bathroom?"

I tried to engage him, explaining that what he was experiencing was completely natural. I explained that we all have to use the bathroom multiple times a day, and he could go right back to playing when he was finished. My son continued to yell, "It's not fair," "Why is everybody doing this to me," "I never get time to play," and "Why are you being so mean to me." I sat down with him for a minute to engage him in a conversation about his heart, explaining that he is complaining about something that cannot be fixed. I also wanted to make sure he understood that I was not being mean. Now, if this story makes you feel like you are not a very patient parent, please don't focus on that. Remember, I said this was my first kid. I had more time and emotional energy to offer this level of patience with my first kid. Now with three kids, these types of conversations are fewer and farther between, and I often have to call-in my husband, Mike, to have those conversations. Give yourself grace.

As I watched this little boy throw a fit about something that seemed so small to me, I didn't understand why my logic wasn't helping. I remember thinking, *Is this really happening? Is my son really so upset about this?* It reminded me of how much I complain about things that are so small in the big picture of God's kingdom, His power, and His providence. Often I complain about not getting enough sleep, how messy my house is, or how seemingly hard finances are to balance, even though God has always provided.

God is not looking at me thinking, *Is this really happening?* Rather He is likely thinking something more like, *child, remember my Word.* In His Word He gave us truth, and sometimes that truth is hard for our human minds to comprehend. I wanted my son to receive my logic and use it to change his emotions. God asks us to turn to His Word in an effort to calm our emotions. Have you ever thought about your emotions that way? Sometimes we behave like small children, stuck on something because of our way of thinking. Yet we have a loving Father who wants us to allow His logic to calm our emotions and change our perspectives. Without the proper perspective, my three-year-old son complained and threw a fit. His little heart felt angry, sad, and stressed. As adults, we are no different. That is the power of perspective.

Biblical Perspectives

The Bible tells us,

> Be alert and of sober mind. Your enemy the devil prowls around like a roaring lion looking for someone to devour.
>
> (1 Peter 5:8)

While sobriety can apply here, this verse communicates far more than what we think of when we think of sobriety from drugs or alcohol. We must have a clear mind. This means we have to pay attention to our thinking, our emotions, and our attitudes in order to have a clear perspective of our situation. Satan wants to confuse us, discourage us, and keep us spinning in circles in negative thinking instead of growing in our relationship with Christ and working toward our God-given purpose.

When we allow our thinking and our perspectives to be misaligned from biblical truth, we get into trouble with how we define our behaviors, who we are, and who others are. A faulty perspective can skew the value we place on our ourselves and our relationships and can taint how we view our purpose in life. If we define those things by an unbiblical view, it can cause significant destruction in our lives. We will miss out on so many blessings that God wants to give us simply because we have allowed the lens through which we see the world to be distorted by unbiblical views. We have to protect our perspectives and not allow the world, our sinful nature, or Satan to fog our thinking and skew our perspectives.

Our Perspectives Can Be Redeemed

When God created humanity, man and woman had a proper understanding and perspective of God. They understood God to be the Creator, Master, and Ruler. But when Adam and Eve allowed Satan to tempt them, and they decided to disobey God and eat the forbidden fruit, it changed their perspective of God. As a result, they also lost their intimate fellowship with Him and each other. Many centuries later, God sent His son Jesus Christ to live a sinless life, and through His death and resurrection, Jesus redeems us from our sinful state whe we believe in Him. Jesus paid our debt of sin, reestablishing our ability to have an intimate relationship with Him.

Friend, I want to encourage you that because of Jesus' sacrifice, you are able to enjoy life-changing intimacy with Christ. Once you commit your life to follow Christ, you should study the Bible so you can continually improve your perspectives of God, yourself, and the world. In doing so, you position yourself to follow Jesus' commands and you submit your thinking and perspective to His truth. Your perspective can be redeemed and sanctified. It takes time as a believer, but in following Christ, the Holy Spirit will convict you and guide you into a Christlike perspective. The joy and freedom that comes with a redeemed perspective is indescribable.

CHAPTER 2

PROPER PERSPECTIVE OF GOD

Gaining a proper perspective of who God is and who you are in relation to Him is the first step in being able to embrace a godly perspective in your life. You have to get to know who the Bible says God is. You cannot follow a Christlike example or have a Christlike perspective if you do not know Jesus Christ personally.

- What do you believe about Jesus?
- Do you believe He was God?
- Do you believe He is in control?
- Do you believe that He is trustworthy?
- Do you believe that He is looking down on you with love or with judgement?
- Do you believe that God cares more about your actions and the rules or your heart and your intentions?
- Do you believe that He has a plan for your life or do you believe that He lets you flounder around as you try to make ends meet?

The foundation to a proper perspective for all areas of your life rests in what you believe about God.

Who is God?

The Bible tells us God is one God in three persons; God the Father, God the Son (Jesus Christ), and God the Holy Spirit. God created the entire universe with a plan to allow humans the choice to follow Him or not. Knowing sin would be introduced, God had a plan for saving humans from their sin by sending His son Jesus to die for our sins. From the beginning, when God created Adam and Eve, He was accessible to humanity. God is still accessible to us today. God takes care of us. He wants a personal relationship with each of us. He comforts us, provides for our needs, and guides us with the Holy Spirit. He is good, wise, gracious, holy, faithful, patient, merciful, righteous, compassionate, trustworthy, and slow to anger. God is omnipotent (all-powerful), omnipresent (everywhere), and omniscient (all-knowing), and He will always remain the same.

God speaks to us personally through His Word, and He comforts us and leads us in decisions through the Holy Spirit. Through prayer, we get to speak to God, and the door to conversation with Him is always open. God exists outside of time, and there is no unit of measure that can contain Him. He punishes the guilty and forgives the believing sinner. He is impartial and saves people regardless of what they have done, are doing, or will do. He is always with us, and He strengthens us in times of need. He chooses us to be His children, and He ordains good works for us to do. God's ways are above our ways—we can never understand His fullness. By God's grace, we have access to Him through faith in Jesus. God defines who we, are and our purpose for living. His Word teaches us how we are to live, think, and perceive the circumstances in which we live.

Jeremiah 10:12, Colossians 1:17, Psalm 147:5, 1 Corinthians 10:13, 1 John 1:5, 2 Ephesians 2:4–5, Peter 3:9, Malachi 3:6, Genesis 1:1, Hebrews 4:12, Job 11:7–11, Jeremiah 23:23–24, Romans 8:35–39, Isaiah 40:23, Hebrews 6:18, James 1:17, John 3:16, Romans 11:33, Matthew 6:26, Eph 2:8–9, Numbers 23:19, Psalm 18:30, Psalm 50:6, Psalm 116:5, Romans 6:23, 1 John 4:7–9, Exodus 34:5–7, Ephesians 3:20, Isaiah 46:9–10, Psalm 137, Psalm 139:7–10, 2 Timothy 2:13, Psalm 34:8, Deuteronomy 32: 4, Romans 9:15–16, Psalm 145:8, Matthew 5:45, Isaiah 41:10, Ephesians 1:4–5, 2 Thessalonians 2: 16–17

If any of the above attributes of God seem foreign to you, I encourage you to look them up and pray about them. Having a proper understanding and perspective of God is foundational. It has power in your life, no matter what trial or tribulation you are facing. As Christ followers, the first step to having a proper perspective in life is having a proper perspective about who God is.

Fear of the Lord

Many Christians know the attributes of God, but oftentimes we miss the crucial detail that Jesus Christ is to be the Lord of our lives. We know that we are supposed to follow Him, believe in Him, and love Him, and while we might know that He is Lord, we don't have much of a concept of what that practically means in our culture. When I explain this concept to my young kids, I have used the term *boss*. I explain to my kids that they are deciding that they want Jesus to be their Lord and Savior—to be their boss—and pay for their sins. I explain to them that if they choose to make Jesus their boss, they will try to follow His rules and believe that He has their best interest in mind.

For many of you, the word *boss* is triggering as you've likely known a boss, or bosses, whom you didn't want to follow. Consider the concept of a boss from a child's perspective. Many times when my kids are arguing, I hear, "You are not my boss." In their minds, a boss is someone who others follow without question, no matter what they say. Do you follow Jesus like that? Have you made Him Lord of your life, or are you still compromising and bending His commands in ways that are likely causing a negative impact on your life? (Hint: Even if it doesn't seem to be negatively impacting your life, it probably is.)

To make Jesus Christ your Lord, you must fear the Lord. Fearing the Lord doesn't mean you are afraid of Him, rather it means that you have a reverence and awe for His authority. If you could visibly see Jesus and His authority with you during every moment of your day, would you make different choices? The truth is that even though you can't visibly see Him, He is very much with you at all times. Would you watch the same shows or mumble the same complaints under your breath? Would you take the same shortcuts at work or speak disrespectfully to your spouse?

Fear of the Lord needs to be your top priority. Fearing God means respecting His authority because you love Him and trust Him. Fearing the Lord means that you make His priorities your priorities and His plans your plans. The deeper your relationship with Jesus, the more you will experience a joy and understanding that your life is His life. As you begin to know Him better, you will begin to feel a greater sense of honor in serving Him because of the purpose and fulfillment He brings to your life. It is important to ask God what His plans are for you.

Since I was young, I have believed that there are many "good" things that I can do with my life, and if I choose the good things then it would be okay. But when I embraced a fear of the Lord, I grew a desire to not just do the "good" things but to seek God's plans for my life. When I ask Him what He wants for my life rather than assuming what I think He wants, I allow for Him to use me in ways that I could never even have imagined for myself, and the blessings of fearing the Lord become a reality.

God's Plan for Our Lives

I was one of those little girls who wanted to be married so badly. When I was in high school, I loved Jesus but I was immature. I did not really understand how to stand up for my faith, and I did not have the maturity to live as a light in a dark world. One of the boys I dated seemed to be Christian enough even though he lacked evidence—or fruit—to support that identity. Though I stood up for some of my convictions, I compromised others because I sought the approval and acceptance of others. I was longing to be precious and important to someone, and because I had a history of being overweight and unpopular, I sacrificed aspects of my faith. I justified my choices by saying to myself, *I'm still young* and *there is still time for me to make God-honoring lifestyle choices later.* I felt like I was "good enough for now." I felt like I was different enough from the way everyone else was living that even my compromised faith should count for something.

During my freshman year of college, I had a wake up call that changed my life forever. At that time I was one of the youth leaders at my church. One day after church there was a youth gathering at a nearby home. Many of the kids carpooled to the gathering that was only a few minutes away from the church. On the way to the house, Josh, our youth pastor's son, was in a car accident. He had three other young people in his car, all who suffered minor injuries. But not Josh. He was killed on impact. The entire youth group, including Josh's family, were within a short distance of the accident when it happened. We had all just seen him alive and well only five short minutes prior to the accident. All of us witnessed moments from that day that remain vivid in our minds. There aren't words to explain the tragedy of that day's devastation as we found out the horrific news together.

Though in shock, I had the presence of mind to spend some time in silence in a quiet room that same day. I remember feeling so small. My mind was flooded with questions about God's presence, purpose, and will for our lives. In the midst of tragedy, it's easy to doubt God and His ways. I tried to offer support to the grieving family, but what is there to say in a moment like that. We were in shock, and the reality of our fragile existence was evident to us all.

As Josh's friend and one of the youth group leaders, I was asked to speak at the funeral. I didn't really have much prepared, and I decided to wing it. While I was speaking, God gave me a perspective that I hadn't seen before. Josh had not been afraid to be light in this dark world. He was two-and-a-half years younger than me but spiritually he was more mature. He brought his Bible with him to a large public school without fear of rejection. He shared the gospel with others because he feared the Lord, and God's kingdom was his priority. As I shared these sentiments at his funeral, I suddenly gained clarity about God's plan for our lives; it was clearer to me in that moment than any other time in my life. Josh was certainly letting his light shine while I was hiding my light under a bushel, as the children's song goes.

As I was sharing this with those who attended his funeral, something inside my heart and my head clicked, and I knew that I could no longer compromise my faith. It fell heavy on my heart that God had a plan for my life.

I wondered that, if it had it been me who died that day, what would others have said about my life? Maybe they would have said the same kinds of things about me as were said of Josh. After all, I had a heart for the Lord, and I volunteered in Mexico and at my church. But the compromise in my heart when I was with my peers weighed heavily as I stood in that moment. I did not understand the important call on a believer's life, a call to be dressed and ready, sober and alert, living a holy and godly life preparing for Jesus's return (Luke 12:35–37, 1 Thessalonians 5 :1–11, 2 Peter 3). Like the switch of a lightbulb, I knew that I did not want to compromise anymore. I wanted God's best plan for my life, not the plan I thought was "good enough for now."

After this life-changing moment, I started surrounding myself with other people who shared my convictions and did not allow me to justify compromising my faith. I took a year-long break from dating as God showed me that I had work to do on myself before I was ready to be married. I spent my time focusing on my identity in Christ instead of focusing on what the world said about me. I stopped looking for approval, acceptance, and value from people, and I started to look for it in Christ alone. In my time with the Lord, I realized that there are many things that we can do that result in "good" and maybe "good enough," but I wanted more. God is our Father, and not only does He know what is best for us, but He also knows what will truly make us happy and healthy.

There is a common fear that God's best for our lives will mean great sacrifice and unhappiness. But He is our loving Father, and He knows that His best is what will make us truly happy. I wanted God's *best* for my life. I was willing to sacrifice whatever He asked, knowing that God would replace my sacrifice with greater fulfillment, spiritual health, and joy in Him. Since then I have been striving for just that.

Friend, we have access to the holy Creator of the universe who knows everything about the past, present, and future. Why wouldn't we seek to find His guidance in our lives instead of making a decision that we think is good? We don't know the future. Our lives could end at any minute of any day. We should not waste time on what we think is good when we could ask God to show us what His best is for us and what His plan is for our lives.

We are created to reflect God and His kingdom in such a remarkable way that other people will see us and know more about Him. We are to reflect God's image to the world. Only God deserves our submission, awe, and lordship over our hearts. For He is the only One who knows the plans for our lives and what will be best for us. Consider what it would look like to let the fear of the Lord override all other influences in your life. If you have a heart that longs to honor God, then let your thoughts, feelings, words, and actions reflect that.

God's Best For Our Lives

I love Proverbs 3:6–8

in all your ways submit to him, and he will make your paths straight. Do not be wise in your own eyes; fear the

Lord and shun evil. This will bring health to your body and nourishment to your bones.

I try to apply those verses to my life in the big and little decisions that I have to make. Do you seek God's will in your decisions?

If you seek God, He will show you which direction to take. The way in which He leads you might look different depending on the decision, but He will lead you in the decisions that will bring about His best for your life. This does not mean that you will be without trials. Even the will of God includes difficulty and hardship with the purpose of growing your faith and refining your weaknesses. Two of the biggest decisions of my life were who to marry and what career to pursue. Your big decisions might be similar to mine or they might be very different. Regardless, you can trust that God will lead you in making the right decision when you seek His best for your life.

When it was time for me to make a decision about marriage, I sensed God's Spirit leading me in my commitment to marriage with Mike. I was certain that Mike was God's best for me. Now more than ever I am certain of that, even though the first few years of our marriage were hard. We both have grown a lot. Making it through those early years of marriage has taught us so much, and we have grown in ways I wouldn't have imagined that I would grow on my own. Mike has added to my life and the ministry calling on my life in ways that would not have been possible without him.

When I sensed that God was calling me to be a Christian counselor, and as I was working toward obeying that call, I had a lot of decisions to make. After finishing graduate school, I interviewed with a few different employers. Two of the potential jobs would allow me to work in a Christian private practice, however, they were part-time positions without a client-base. I assumed that either of those jobs would be the means to my end goal, but God had other plans. Two other job opportunities offered me full-time work with benefits, but I could not practice Christian counseling at all. These opportunities were in a secular setting. I agonized over what to do because I knew my end goal was to practice Christian counseling. After praying a lot and seeking advice, and because of the reality of our financial circumstances at the time, I decided that God was leading me to take the full-time community counseling job with benefits. My plan was to someday start a private practice in which I could ensure that counseling was offered from a biblical worldview rather than a worldly one. Accepting the full-time job with benefits allowed me a more stable path toward my end goal.

If I had made the job decision on my own without seeking the Lord's guidance, I would have assumed that the Christian counseling position was what I should do since a Christian practice was the end goal. I almost accepted that job. But I felt led to take a different path, and in doing so, I met another therapist, Bridget, who is now my business partner. The two of us formed a team that eventually included Mike. He was able to offer his skill-set and experience to manage the operations and marketing for our business. I was not wise enough to foresee how God would orchestrate this situation; I could not have dreamt it. But God knew, and our team of three is more than a dream come true. Following God's lead and asking for Him to guide my steps in His best for my life has been one of the most important lessons I have ever learned.

Knowing that I am a child of God and called according to His purpose made it easy to believe that He has a best plan for my life.

Since God is all-knowing, patient, and sovereign, He knows just how to get my attention to follow His leading. And if you are looking for His leading, He will get your attention too.

Friend, I want to encourage you to consider how your definition of God has affected how you see the world and yourself. Consider areas in which you may need to change how you see God. Without a proper perspective of God and your identity in Him, you will struggle to discern His leading. Do you know who God is? Do you know who you are in relation to Him? When you have a proper perspective of God, you can start to develop a proper perspective of yourself and your identity because God defines our identity and our worth.

CHAPTER 3

PROPER PERSPECTIVE OF OURSELVES

Once you embrace a proper perspective of God, you can start to develop a proper perspective of yourself. These two things are intertwined, so if you struggle with one the other will suffer. It is important to know that we can go to God for the truth. The sinfulness of other people and the lies of Satan are oftentimes interpreted as truth that we allow to define ourselves.

We develop our understanding of who we are early in life. As infants, we learn whether we can trust the world and others. In fact, secular psychology has identified that people can struggle with shame as young as one and a half years old, guilt as young as three years old, and inferiority as young as five years old. All of these stages start to define how we see ourselves. If these early beliefs about ourselves are negative, they can result in many years of inner turmoil, including an adverse perception of self, an inability to accept God's love, and even chronic depression.

Developing Identity

Our identity is a psychosocial construct. This means that our identity is developed in the context of relationship. The social interactions we have with others, the beliefs that others have about us, and the way the world defines us all collide to define how we see ourselves. When we have an experience, the information we receive from that experience is processed through our perspective and then added to our definition of ourselves. You can think of this concept as if you were looking into a metaphorical mirror your entire life to define who is there looking back at you. Based on your experiences, by the time you are five you may already have cracks in your mirror filled with feelings such as shame, guilt, or inferiority. If no one helps you determine that those negative experiences do not define who you are, the cracks will continue to grow.

The more you experience peer rejection, failure, stress in the home, and other psychosocial challenges, the more cracks develop. The longer those cracks exist without being corrected and fixed by God's truths, the deeper those cracks in your mirror become. Often by the time we are teenagers we have enough cracks in the mirror that our reflection is no longer clear. This timing is crucial because developmentally, teenagers are trying to define themselves outside of their family's definition of themselves. These cracks can exacerbate an already confusing time.

Even though my parents tried their best to make sure that I knew I was loved by them and by God, my childhood was often tough. I was rejected by peers, and I was singled out in the classroom as the loner with very few friends. I had an easier time working one-on-one, but in groups I felt isolated. As a young girl, I started to have cracks in the reflection I saw in my mirror. When I was in high school, I struggled with my worth and my identity in Christ. God blessed me with a very supportive family, but the rejection I encountered from peers greatly impacted how I viewed myself. It was easy for me to beat myself up and be self-critical. Even though I had a Christian foundation, I still allowed peers and my own negative thoughts to contribute to my identity. When I looked in my mirror to define myself, I believed the lies that I was unliked, unloved, defective, ugly, stupid, and a failure.

Ultimately, I corrected this way of thinking, but it was hard work. The good news is that since your identity is defined in the context of relationship, your relationship with Jesus can heal the distortions in your perception that were created in relationships with people. To start, I had to identify the cracks in my mirror and who I had defined myself to be. Then I had to dig deep and strengthen my understanding of who I was in Christ. I spent time in the Word of God to learn what my mirror should be showing me. I spent time with mentors and in Christian counseling to determine where my perspective was misaligned because I wasn't even aware of where the cracks were in the mirror that were causing the image I saw of myself to be so distorted. The journey was a hilly one. Many times, I would begin to understand the truth about my identity in Christ, but then life circumstances or trials would bring something back up and I would doubt myself again.

Even today, if my husband says something in the wrong tone and it pushes on one of those lies I believed about myself, I go right back into the negative thoughts about who I am. It takes intentional effort to bring myself back to truth quickly. Figuring out how to firmly embrace your identity in Christ can be a lifelong lesson that ebbs and flows. The good news is that once you understand this and accept it, the default toward the negative begins to lessen and you can start to see a clear, hope-filled reflection in your mirror instead of a distorted image that comes from a broken mirror.

The more you practice replacing the lies you believe about yourself with the truths of your identity in Christ, the easier it gets to make that shift.

- What do you see when you look in your metaphorical mirror? Do you believe the lies from childhood that you are unliked or unloved? Do you see someone who is defective or a failure?
- Do you believe the lies of Satan who tried to oppose every part of God's truth?

You are not a slave to your past or how others define you. With the wrong perspective, you will experience self-rejection, self-condemnation, unhappiness, anxiety, unrest, depression, and the list goes on. This is why there is power in having the proper perspective about your identity and your worth. You cannot experience joy from the Lord without understanding your identity as a redeemed follower of Christ.

Self-image

Our thoughts and feelings about ourselves can shape our perspectives of ourselves. Psychology would label our view of self as our self-image. Having a biblical self-image is another foundational component to having a proper perspective on other things in our lives.

If we have a <u>deflated self-image</u> then we think lowly of ourselves in an unhealthy way, taking away our motivation and energy. We view ourselves as unable to keep up with others, and we will often feel depressed and defeated. We will lean toward self-defeat. We will put boundaries around what we can accomplish, and we will not push ourselves to reach a higher potential.

If we have a <u>negative self-image</u> then we focus on our weaknesses. We are prone to comparing the worst of ourselves with the best of others (this is so easy to do now thanks to social media). This will make us feel anxious and unhappy. It will predispose us to failure and self-sabotage and selfish thinking.

If we have an <u>inflated self-image,</u> then we think we are actually better than most people. This will often leave us feeling frustrated with others. It will make it hard to relate to other people, and we will have little compassion and grace. It will allow pride to grow in our hearts and lead us to a lack of understanding for our need for God's strength in our weaknesses (Philippians 2:3–4).

If we have a <u>positive self-image</u> then we will see our positives, and we will strive to meet our potential. We are more likely to give grace to others, and we will operate out of peace and joy. A positive self-image is healthy, but without an eternal perspective, we may lack purpose and miss out on godly joy.

Your self-image can fluctuate between the different views of self based on your situation or in regard to different areas of life. However, I would advocate for working toward a biblical view of self, which I have named a <u>redeemed self-image</u>. If we have a <u>redeemed self-image</u> then we have humility in the sight of God and an understanding of His love for us. We live aware of our value to God. We have a positive self-image but we also have a healthy assessment of self. We know our personal shortcomings and weaknesses, and we know that as believers, God works things together for our good. We strive to be who God created us to be through spending time with Him in prayer, personal study of His Word, taking part in Christian community, and sitting under biblical teaching. We can remain positive when facing our failures knowing that God has something new to refine in us each day. (James 4:4–10, 1 Peter 5:6, Galatians 4:6–7, Romans 8:14–17, Romans 12:3)

No matter what view of self you tend to believe, a redeemed self-image is available to you. Regardless of your shortcomings and no matter what aspects of your personality you or others don't like, God redeems as we search our hearts. God transforms our identities by renewing our minds through Scripture and through the Holy Spirit's work in us. I cannot stress enough the importance of self-reflection in developing a healthy perspective of life.

> For by the grace given me I say to every one of you: Do not think of yourself more highly than you ought, but rather think of yourself with sober judgment, in accordance with the faith God has distributed to each of you.
>
> (Romans 12:3)

Most of my job as a thearpist has been teaching people how to self-reflect about their thoughts, feelings, attitudes, motives, and needs in order to better embrace a healthier perspective.

Biblical View of Self

To develop a biblical view of self, it is important to have a proper perspective even about the negative things we think of ourselves. We need to first acknowledge them, and then we can allow the Holy Spirit to help us dissolve them and replace them with His truths. The things in which we view as negative about ourselves, God calls our *flesh*. Facing these negative things can seem burdensome or depressing from our human perspective, but from

God's perspective, these weaknesses give us the opportunity to allow God's power to strengthen us. If we could do it all on our own, then we would not see our need for God. Paul explains this in his letter to the Corinthians.

> But He said to me, "My grace is sufficient for you, for my power is made perfect in weakness." Therefore I will boast all the more gladly about my weaknesses, so that Christ's power may rest on me. That is why, for Christ's sake, I delight in weaknesses, in insults, in hardships, in persecutions, in difficulties. For when I am weak, then I am strong.
>
> (2 Corinthians 12:9–10)

Our weaknesses are a big part of who we are, but the Bible does not stop there in defining our identity. You cannot get stuck exclusively on your negatives. Acknowledge your weaknesses with the perspective that you are a work in progress. Remember who you are now is not who you will be next year as long as you allow the Holy Spirit to work in you.

> being confident of this, that he who began a good work in you will carry it on to completion until the day of Christ Jesus.
>
> (Philippians 1:6)

Just like the story of the ugly duckling in which a strange-looking bird who counts himself out, later blooms into a beautiful swan, we also change, grow, and transform as we go through life. It's okay, and maybe even helpful, to acknowledge the negatives, but focus your thoughts on the positives and who God is molding you to become.

> Finally, brothers and sisters, whatever is true, whatever is noble, whatever is right, whatever is pure, whatever is lovely, whatever is admirable—if anything is excellent or praiseworthy—think about such things.
>
> (Philippians 4:8)

The Bible tells us many positive things about our identity. The closer we walk with Him, the easier it is to embrace a redeemed self-image and keep our minds focused on things worthy of praise. The Bible tells us we are unique and wonderfully made. It tells us that we are flawed by our sin but redeemed, we are fully dependent on God, we are created in God's image (Genesis 1:27), and we are dearly loved. When God was explaining His love for Israel, He said:

> Since you are precious and honored in my sight, and because I love you, I will give people in exchange for you, nations in exchange for your life.
>
> (Isaiah 43:4)

Every believer is precious and loved by Christ (Ephesians 3:14–19). I always longed to feel precious. I think God intentionally made this part of the young girl's heart to draw us to Him. Even in popular children's movies, girls long to be precious to someone. We are precious to God. We are created for a high calling and for a highly important purpose.

Friend, take a moment to consider this. God loves you so much and created you with your unique talents, abilities, and skills. He has allowed you to experience the ups and downs in your life so that you would be prepared to fulfill a unique purpose that would play a role in God's overall divine plan for the world. You are indescribably valuable and important to your heavenly Creator.

Jesus saved us from our sin, and if that was His only plan for us then He would have taken us up to heaven right then. He left us here on earth to help others, to make an impact on the world, and to bring others to Christ. No matter your weaknesses, trials or ailments, if you are still breathing, God has a plan for you. He is not finished with you, and He has so much more in store for you. Don't waste your time here on earth with a negative perspective of yourself. Let your relationship with Jesus fix the cracks in your mirror so you can see a clear image of the indescribably valuable person that is looking back at you.

Changing Your Perspective

All this sounds nice, but life is challenging. Trials come our way and we lose our footing. We cower before our spiritual enemy, even when we don't realize this is what is happening. We feel overwhelmed, discouraged, depressed, and condemned. We feel like we are stuck in a miserable rut and we must dig ourselves out before God can make progress with us. We try to do it on our own, but we don't realize that our rut is now deepening as we keep digging in the wrong directions. We do this because we are basing our worth on 1) Satan's lies, 2) our past experiences with other broken and sinful people and 3) our feelings about our flesh. We base our worth on these things instead of basing our worth on the true, honorable, right, and scriptural facts of who God is, what He accomplished through the cross, and who we are as followers of Christ.

So if you are stuck on Satan's lies, your negative experiences, or feelings of your flesh, how can you change your perspective and see your worth through the redeeming power of Christ? It starts with hearing the truth, and hearing the truth, and hearing the truth, over and over again. Remember who you are in Christ. You are a child of God, dearly loved and called according to His purpose. Use references of who you are in Christ to give you a clear picture of who you are. Some people say not to ask who you are but whose you are. This is a similar concept.

Pray that you will be able to let go of negative experiences and destructive self-talk. Consider reaching out to a friend or a Christian counselor to process and talk through these things. Sometimes when we say things out loud, the power those experiences and lies have over us begins to break.

It helps to talk about it with someone who will challenge your negative thoughts. External processing is an advantage in this area as long as your sounding board does not discourage you or stir up an unbiblical perspective. The more we allow our thoughts inside our heads to continue spinning around, the more we give them power to control our thinking and define our perspective on life. Sometimes just hearing our thoughts out loud helps us understand how our thoughts and words can contradict biblical truth.

I also suggest finding a preacher with whom you connect. Find a sermon series on the issue with which you are struggling and listen to it. There is also power in hearing the truth out loud that helps it sink deep into the heart. Another thing that has helped me a lot is to find worship music that encourages my heart with specific truths that I am struggling to believe. Find worship music and sing to it regularly. Let the words shower your soul with the truth of God's Word (John 4:24).

Something that has made a big difference in my life was a result of my attendance in a weekly Bible study called Bible Study Fellowship (BSF). BSF is an amazing international ministry for men and women, with locations in most major cities in the United States. BSF focuses on studying one book of the Bible each year. After a few years of attending BSF, I began to pray that God would help me to learn about His Word in such a way that it would make a difference in my life. Even though I missed some of the lessons when my kids were sick, and even though I wasn't the perfect Bible study student, God honored my prayer.

Year after year, the truths I was learning in BSF began to take root in my heart and in my life. With a heart willing to listen and learn, I began to experience new insights about God in relation to my life. Each year, as I studied the Scriptures, God highlighted a theme for me. This theme highlighted a perspective issue with which I was unknowingly struggling. Once God revealed to me the highlighted theme, it reinforced what He was trying to teach me by finding a complementary worship song and listening to it on repeat.

One year the song that stuck with me was about God's presence. Another year the song was about God's beauty and the eternal perspective of uniting with Him in heaven. Another year the song that stuck with me was about Jesus' death on the cross and the love He showed us through His sacrifice. I wasn't looking for these songs but God helped me find them. I started singing these songs to my kids every night before bed, and over time, I felt my soul transform. Singing about the truth made it easier to allow God to transform my perspective. It changed how I felt about life, how I understood things, and how I thought about things. It changed the filter with which I process new information. Worship music was like medicine. Each night as I sang to my kids, the truth that the Holy Spirit highlighted for me pressed deeper and deeper into my soul.

- Who can you talk to about your negative thoughts?
- On what do you base your worth?
- Do you know whose you are?
- Do you spend time hearing God's truth regularly?
- What Christian songs encourage you?

CHAPTER 4

EMBRACING AN ETERNAL PERSPECTIVE

Most of us live focused on our day-to-day lives—our to-do lists, work obligations, household responsibilities, family demands, or a friend's needs. It's easy to get bogged down by our daily rhythms and forget about our purpose here on earth. The Bible tells us that we are not simply living for this life but we are living for our life after death. We are to share the gospel so that others can join us in eternity with Jesus. If you are a follower of Christ, you are guaranteed an eternity with Jesus and other believers. Eternity is the purpose of our life here on earth.

The concept of our eternal purpose for this life was one of the most significant lessons I learned to remedy the stresses, anxieties, and negative feelings in my life. If you have committed your life to follow Jesus and have a relationship with Him, you have access to His transforming insights through an eternal perspective. The biggest help in having a proper perspective is keeping eternity at the center.

An eternal perspective understands that the purpose of our lives on earth is to bring glory to God and win souls for Christ by living out our calling in God's kingdom. The Bible has a lot to say about God's plan for our lives as believers including: He will provide for our daily needs (Matthew 6:31–33). He will provide you with the Holy Spirit as a helper (John 14:26). He gives you a chosen role in His kingdom to further His work on earth (1 Corinthians 12:18). He will provide you with spiritual strength (Ephesians 3:14,16). He will provide you a way out of temptation (1 Corinthians 10:13). He will provide you with His joy (John 15:11). He will provide you with what you need in order to do His will and to fulfill His calling on your life (Hebrews 13:20–21). He will provide us with eternal protection (Hebrews 13:6). He will provide us with abundant blessings whether in this life or throughout eternity (Mark 10:29–30). One day we will be with Him (John 14:2–3). One day His work in us will be completed (Philippians 1:6). One day we will be like Jesus when we meet Him in eternity (1 John 3:2). He will wipe away the tears from our eyes (Revelation 21:6). Death is not the end. We have been promised an abundant and eternal life. Even when death comes in this life, nothing can threaten us or bring us eternal harm (1 Thessalonians 4:13).

Do you live like you believe these things about God, yourself, and eternity? Having an eternal perspective means you believe that there is a bigger purpose to your existence than what you can visibly see before you. It means believing that there is a reason for your struggles and your blessings. It means that God is in control and will work everything out for your good according to His eternal purposes (Romans 8:28).

Knowing these truths means that we can embrace God's peace in our daily lives knowing that there is a purpose to the grind, the easy days and the difficult days. We can embrace a confidence in knowing that God's plans are bigger and better than our plans.

These truths are an invitation to discover opportunities to bring glory to God through our lives.

Surrendering to God's Plans

I have always been someone with a chip of responsibility on my shoulders, even as a kid. I found it hard to have fun when I was a teenager because I was worried about what could happen if I failed to consider the consequences of every action. When I compared myself to what my friends were doing, I seemed to be too responsible. Although there were some downsides to this chip of responsibility (it was hard for me to relax, and I was always putting pressure on myself to do things with excellence), it has mostly served me well in life.

Looking back, I accomplished the things I set out to accomplish. I became a therapist, I started a practice, I had three kids, and now I am writing a book. That being said, my body has taken a physical beating with so much cortisol (the stress hormone) pumping through my veins as I worked hard, slept little, stressed a lot, and pressed on. At times I neglected to turn off my active brain in order to rest and find balance. A feeling of too much responsibility made it very hard to look up and have an eternal perspective. Often I was looking down at myself and the many little things I was doing, or not doing, ALL the time.

I was so stressed out. I was so caught up in feeling like God had given me too big of a puzzle to solve, too many burdens to bear, and too many details to manage. In our business, we spent years just trying to survive because making money through our counseling practice seemed impossible and adding new babies every few years always brought with it more work and responsibility than we expected. In those years I know that Mike got the last little remnants of what was left of me, and my kids did not get the attention I wanted to give them. It wasn't until I started learning how to have an eternal perspective that I could have some peace about the plans God has for me and the calling He placed on my life. Once I made that shift, I was better able to spend more time engaged with my family.

Shortly after starting our counseling business with my wonderful co-founder, who is also a talented therapist, Mike and I sought God's direction in order to find balance for our family. God helped us understand that, for the health of our family, I needed to figure out a way to let go of the burden of carrying so much weight related to the success of the business. Mike had another job at the time and worked hard to take over that burden, but we both felt God was prompting Mike to quit his job and give his full-time attention to the business operations of the counseling practice. This was terrifying as the business was still not making enough money to pay me a consistent salary, not to mention also pay Mike. But we trusted God and took the leap of faith. Through government assistance, family support, and other surprising and unexpected ways, God provided for us.

Worrying about how things would work out was one of my biggest struggles at the time. Even though it is still a struggle at times and my flesh tries to pull me back into overdrive as I analyze the cash flow, profit margins, and patterns of growth, I have learned to better experience God's peace as I trust His plans for our business and for our family. Having Mike oversee operations has helped ease the burden, and it has given our family greater balance. Figuring out how to organize our life in the healthiest way for us could only have been done by seeking the Lord's direction.

Owning your own business is a lot of responsibility, and it makes it hard to remember that God is in control. Being entrepreneurs, we have learned to seek God's directions often for our businesses and what His next steps are for us. Starting a business is stressful and for many months, ends did not meet, but I learned something important during the stressful time. I learned many ways God provides for us outside of the conventional ways. Not only did I learn to trust God with our finances, I also learned that no matter our situation, an eternal perspective of God's plan for our lives and for our business was and is the only way that I will experience true rest and true peace.

An eternal perspective allows me to be thankful and honored for the blessing of running our own business, a business with an eternal mission of reaching those who need Christ's healing in their lives. We could not be doing any of the work we do without God. Our business is His business.

Just because I learned this lesson doesn't mean I never struggle with fear about God's plans and provision. Many important lessons are learned over and over again. I have to work hard to fight feeling like a failure every time we try one more new thing in hopes to increase profits only for it to not work out. It requires great intentionality to shake the sting of another lost investment. We try to seek the Lord in all that we do, and even if we end up failing, we always learn something important.

It is imperative that we are always ready to make business decisions as problems often arise. Sometimes the changes we make put stress on our staff, and in turn makes our burden of ownership feel even heavier. Sometimes we are just in survival mode.

The only way I survive being a Christian entrepreneur long term is to get to a place of surrendering control of our business and our lives to Christ.

I am still learning to surrender. I need to surrender the notion that it is solely up to me to make our employees happy, and I need to surrender the desire to ensure that our valuable staff is compensated competitively. I have to surrender people's opinions and needs. I need to surrender the push back from the market, and I have to surrender feeling like it's up to me to figure out how to survive. I must surrender the worry that when the next therapist leaves their clients will have to suffer the feeling of abandonment and starting over. I have to surrender the constant anxiety that comes with making a business successful, and I have to surrender the pressure of a high risk industry with slim margins and profit–loss ratios that fluctuate rapidly beyond our control due to third party reimbursement limits.

Surrendering it all to God makes the heaviness feel light. It has to be intentional, and I have to work at this perspective every day. If I do not surrender, I am unable to keep an eternal perspective that God is in control, that He will provide for our staff and for us, that He will care for our clients, and that this business is really His business.

An in-depth study of Revelation helped me to grasp that my life, and our business, was only a small piece of the eternal puzzle. I felt that God called me to Christian counseling when I was young as I was always a good listener and curious about people's lives. I genuinely cared about what other people were thinking, and I had a natural desire to help them solve their problems. During one time of doubting I had to ask myself, if it was His calling, wouldn't

He take care of me? Beyond what I can see, God has a larger plan. He deeply desires to reach the lost and heal the broken. Since our clients who request a Christian perspective in therapy can receive healing on a soul level and our clients who do not request a Christian perspective can at least see the Bible verses on our walls each week, then isn't it worth the risk and investment of building this business? When I reframe the purpose of our practice and my life through an eternal perspective, I begin to realize that all the years of sweat and tears created something that God has blessed.

Your situation differs from mine. Maybe you are a stay-at-home parent or maybe you are a work-from-home parent or maybe you work 50 hours a week and have several part-time jobs. Maybe you are married or maybe you are single. Maybe you are widowed. Maybe you have kids or maybe you cannot have kids. No matter what your situation is, whatever it is that brings you stress, if God has called you to it, He will provide you with what you need to do it. He has a plan for your life, and even if you are in a rough patch, you can find peace by looking up to Jesus and believing that He is not done with you yet. Your story is not yet complete. When completion arrives, we already know the ending: We will be fully sanctified, living with our Lord Jesus Christ. Our tears will be washed away. This is the reality of an eternal perspective.

Finding Peace in an Eternal Perspective

If you can embrace an understanding of God's bigger purpose, you will begin to reframe the situations in your life and you will start to experience a peace that you have never known before. So how do you find that perspective? How can you search your heart and lay down your plans for your life to make room for His plans?

You may have to do some deep internal work with God, answering questions that maybe you never asked yourself before. My life is an ongoing arena for this internal work. I have to wrestle with myself often to keep the fears and stubbornness of my flesh in submission with Christ. When things get hard, when plans fall through, when I feel out of control, when I feel afraid of the future, or when I lose a sense of peace, God is there and ready to meet with me.

Like me, He will meet with you in those times of need. The Holy Spirit will provide comfort and strength, and He will guide you in the way you should go. All of this and more is available to you, but only if you are postured toward Him by spending time in prayer, reading God's Word, taking your thoughts captive, surrendering your will, and seeking the heart of Jesus for your life.

The Apostle Paul gives us a clear example of the peace that an eternal perspective provides us when he speaks to the Ephesian elder in Acts chapter 20.

> When they arrived, he said to them: "You know how I lived the whole time I was with you, from the first day I came into the province of Asia. I served the Lord with great humility and with tears and in the midst of severe testing by the plots of my Jewish opponents. You know that I have not hesitated to preach anything that would be helpful to you but have taught you publicly and from house to house. I have declared to both Jews and Greeks that they must turn to God in repentance and have faith in our Lord Jesus. "And now, compelled by the Spirit, I am going to Jerusalem, not knowing what will happen to me there. I only know that in every city the Holy Spirit warns

me that prison and hardships are facing me. However, I consider my life worth nothing to me; my only aim is to finish the race and complete the task the Lord Jesus has given me—the task of testifying to the good news of God's grace.

(Acts 20:18–24)

The Bible tells us that everything good is from God (James 1:17), and "in all things God works for the good of those who love him, who have been called according to his purpose" (Romans 8:28). Since I believe the Bible is truth, I had to ask myself, if I truly love Jesus and have surrendered my life to Him, then am I willing to follow Him wherever He takes me?

I had to decide if I was willing to find peace and joy in stress and even in suffering because I know that the purpose of my life is to bring glory to God. This world is not our home, so I had to decide if I was willing to be happy with being a little uncomfortable in this world so that His plan for my life will prevail.

After wrestling with my thoughts, I concluded that the answers to these are yes I will follow Him and yes I will willingly find peace and happiness in stress and discomfort for the glory of His kingdom.

It was difficult to answer yes with my whole heart to those questions; it took some soul searching. My faith in Jesus had to overpower my pride in order to surrender. I still struggle with slipping back into a timid "yes" or even sometimes "maybe" when my pride fights back, but when I have time to reconnect with Jesus, I can surrender my fleshly human preferences and live with an eternal perspective.

To have a peace that surpasses understanding (Philippians 4:7) you need to remain focused on an understanding that the purpose of your life is to grow God's eternal kingdom. You must remember this in the day-to-day grind of work, kids, school, chores, errands, and relationships. It is also important to remember this in times of support or opposition. We must keep in mind the following:

> And we know that in all things God works for the good of those who love him, who have been called according to his purpose.
>
> (Romans 8:28)

It's important to keep in mind that God has a purpose even in our daily mundane tasks.

- Will you follow Jesus wherever He takes you with a peace and joy that only comes from knowing that God is in control?
- What will you decide about your suffering?

Finding Peace in Suffering

Anyone who has ever tried to have a Christlike perspective knows how hard this can be, especially in times of suffering. Even when we think we have our thoughts right, life invades our perspectives and our pain takes over. We begin seeing things again as the world tells us we should or we begin to lie to ourselves, denying that we are struggling. As humans our automatic responses are typically to maximize comfort and minimize pain; however, when we do this we actually avoid spiritual and emotional growth. This ironically leads to more pain and stress and less peace and joy.

Friend, whether we are in a season of suffering or thriving or anywhere in between, God has a purpose for today. In times of prosperity and in times of need, God has a purpose for each season. To fully embrace a God-given peace, trust in God's plans for your life and grasp God's sovereignty. Consider the following:

For I know the plans I have for you," declares the Lord, "plans to prosper you and not to harm you, plans to give you hope and a future.

(Jeremiah 29:11)

To understand the full promise of plans not to harm you in Jeremiah 29, it is important to first understand the context of this verse. Some think that this verse means that God will not make you suffer for a very long period of time. Some think that this verse speaks to the idea that God won't give you more than you can handle. However most scholars and theologians agree that although God doesn't allow people to be tempted beyond what they can handle, suffering is a different story. Not to mention, I have seen many, many people in my counseling office who have been given more than they can handle. However, what is true is that God can handle it. Jesus has already handled it, and the Holy Spirit will give you the strength to keep going when your circumstances feel like they are too much. In our weakness, He is strong.

As for Jeremiah 29:11, the Israelites were told that they would prosper, and God followed through on that promise…70 years later! It was 70 years before the suffering ended for the Israelites. Most of the people in the generation who first heard the words of the prophet Jeremiah did not even live long enough to see the promise fulfilled. The same can be true for us. Sometimes we do not get to see the fullness of God's promises within our lifetimes. Not until eternity will we experience complete prosperity, and some of us will know suffering until our final breath.

Everyone has encountered their share of stress, anxiety, wounding, and pain. In the counseling field, we encounter those who are brave enough to ask for help. Typically, our clients have either suffered in the past or they are presently suffering, and many times they have lived with suffering longer than they have lived without it.

Therapists see pain in the eyes of small children who have endured sexual abuse or the loss of parents. We see the desperation of parents who have lost their children to addiction. We see the trauma caused by spousal betrayal. We see the hurt that comes to families through divorce, mental illness or poverty.

When I was still relatively new to the field of counseling, I couldn't kick a feeling of hopelessness. I asked the question, "Since bad things happen to good people, and God allows people to endure suffering beyond what most people can handle, then where is the hope? And how does all of this fit with God's promise to unconditionally love all people?"

These questions led me to spending intense and intentional time with God to find answers. After a while of pursuing God for answers, I started to see hope. I started to understand. To understand, I had to slowly surrender my fleshly desire of wanting to avoid pain and remain comfortable and cozy in my life. I learned how to think about trials as Christ thinks about them.

The purpose of our lives is to bring glory to God and to win souls for Christ. God protects us from some things, probably so much more than we even know, but He lets other things happen, even things that make no sense to us.

> Therefore, since Christ suffered in his body, arm your-selves also with the same attitude, because whoever suffers in the body is done with sin. As a result, they do not live the rest of their earthly lives for evil human desires, but rather for the will of God.
>
> (1 Peter 4:1–2)

Experiencing my own times of suffering while also seeing the suffering of others, I was forced to put it into perspective. I have learned that many of the things that God allows are consequences of living in a sinful world and it is not punishment or something that God does to us. God does allow some things to happen while protecting us from others. Maybe God allows difficult things to happen knowing that in our suffering we have the opportunity to draw closer to Him. When we and others are drawn to Him, God's glory prevails.

Through a proper understanding of God, and through a deeper level of intimacy with Him, we can experience peace amidst our suffering. The personal life changes that come with knowing God at a deeper level are evidence of God's strength in your weakness. As others watch the outcome of a deeper reliance on God through the suffering you endure, God is glorified.

If the purpose of our lives is to bring glory to Him with a wholly surrendered heart, shouldn't we be willing to endure whatever hardships are necessary to amplify God's glory? In this question, consider John 10:10. The Enemy wants to kill, steal and destroy us to cause our suffering. God wants to give us life abundantly!

> The thief comes only to steal and kill and destroy; I have
> come that they may have life, and have it to the full.
>
> (John 10:10)

Go to God in your suffering. God hears our concerns, and He knows the pain that we endure. No matter the suffering, He is always compassionate. It's not about us. We live in a sinful world because of the fall of man. Sometimes we reap what we sow, but other times we suffer the consequences of someone else's sin. In some capacity or another, we are all suffering from the decay of this world (Ephesians 12:3–11).

When I am working with clients who are suffering, it helps me to remember that God is our Father. God is alongside us in our suffering (Psalm 34:18). If we can remember that our lives are indescribably small in comparison to eternity (James 4:14), we can have a better perspective on our suffering. When this life is over it won't matter how much pain we endured nor will it matter what we acquired or accomplished for worldly gain while we were alive. Instead what matters is whether or not we fully surrendered to God and followed His call.

Peace Regardless of your Prosperity

Returning to Jeremiah 29:11, what if God's idea of prosperity is different than your Americanized idea of prosperity? If we consider this verse in light of the American dream, then we will be confused when our wealth or our health is threatened. If we lose our home, if our bank account is in the red, or if we encounter chronic illness, how do we reconcile the promise God makes in Jeremiah 29:11? Here's the thing. God takes care of us, but that doesn't mean that we will always have our own car, a nice house, fancy vacations, extra money to redecorate, or perfect health. So what perspective should we have about God's provision in light of this verse?

For about four years we were constantly trying to answer the question, "Is our business viable?" After living under the constant fear that one day we would lose everything, I had to change my perspective. God helped me to see this in a special way. I felt Him put a directive on my heart. I had the thought, *Let your bank account go to zero and then watch what I can do.* Our account went to zero for a short time but ever since, God has come through every month, even when the outlook was grim. God took the investment we made into the business, and He used it to grow our business faster than we ever thought possible. Our margins are still slim, but we have been able to impact more lives than I ever dreamed. We are making an eternal impact in the Kingdom of God. I realized I had to stop thinking that we were merely surviving, and I had to start remembering that God has a plan for our business, our family, and our lives. I had to decide that only God knows our future, so I was going to trust Him.

God provides us with everything that we need to do the work He has called us to do.

So what if all of a sudden you have no job and no money?
God will provide.
What if you have little to nothing saved for your kid's college?
God will provide.
What if you get sued and have to file bankruptcy?

God will provide.

What if you have to sell your house and live with family?

God will provide.

What if you let go of control and fully surrender all of your fears to God? *He will take your life and make it into something more beautiful than you could have imagined.* You will bring more souls to Christ and glory to His name just by being faithful because that is the true purpose of our lives.

I have learned that God knows what we will need now and in the future. He knows what kind of medical bills we will have in our older years. He knows how long we will live. He knows if our families will get to use the life insurance policy or if Christ will return before our lifetime is over. If He is all-knowing and if He is all-powerful, then we can release the weight of responsibility and follow His lead on what to do next. We can do that with a heart and soul that rests on Him.

Being able to grasp that reality has helped me be much less stressed about money and life. Though I still have a sinful flesh that I have to put to death daily, and though I often forget about eternity, I plan to reread this chapter often so that I can more easily straighten my perspective when it becomes skewed. If I can keep an eternal perspective, I can understand that I am not living for today, nor am I living for ten years from now, nor twenty years from now. I'm not even living for retirement. I am living solely for eternity.

CHAPTER 5

PROPER PERSPECTIVE OF OTHERS

An important part of our lives is our relationships with other people. Many variables impact our relationships such as, past relationships, self-esteem, and experiences we have had. These variables compound to form our perspectives about others. Past relationships affect how we see current relationships, and how we see other people affects how we relate to them.

God created us to be in relationship with Himself and other people. Our relationships with others do not define us because God defines us, but learning how to unconditionally love others just as God loves us unconditionally is part of His plan for the relationships in our lives. Being a sinful person who has relationships with other sinful people is challenging. When relationships are healthy, God's purpose is for us to encourage each other, sharpen our faith, strengthen each other, serve and support each other, and show love to each other. Also, relationships are the best context for us to share Christ with non-believers. Given their importance, Satan does all he can to bring about strife, misunderstandings, and unhealthy habits in our relationships. He can hinder the blessing of relationships in our lives when we misinterpret, feel offended, or harbor negative feelings toward others.

Our perspective plays a role in how we interpret other people's opinions and intentions. Our interpretation then affects how we see other people. It is easy for us to develop an unhealthy understanding of how relationships should function, how we should feel about other people in certain situations, and at what point we should give up on having a healthy relationship with someone. To have healthy relationships, we need a mindset of compassion.

We often judge people's actions and words without giving them grace. But we don't know what people are going through when they cut us off on the road or when they don't smile back at us in the store. We need to hold onto the understanding that they may be on their own sanctification journey. The ways in which God has convicted you may not be at the same pace that He has convicted someone else. There are certain personalities that will rub us the wrong way, but I do believe that a believer with a grace-filled perspective can get along with almost anyone.

Embracing Compassion

It is easy to be annoyed with other people when they need something from us, when they inconvenience us, or when they seem rude. We all experience being irritated with others from time to time, and usually we have that experience without really thinking about it. We often develop expectations of what other people should do or say or how they should think. When people don't meet those expectations, we have a negative experience of them. But is there a way that we can experience those same seemingly irritating people without actually feeling irritated? What if I told you that you absolutely can, and it's all a matter of perspective?

Do nothing out of selfish ambition or vain conceit. Rather, in humility value others above yourselves, not looking to your own interests but each of you to the interests of the others.

(Philippians 2:3–4)

Hold them in the highest regard in love because of their work. Live in peace with each other. And we urge you, brothers and sisters, warn those who are idle and disruptive, encourage the disheartened, help the weak, be patient with everyone. Make sure that nobody pays back wrong for wrong, but always strive to do what is good for each other and for everyone else.

(1 Thessalonians 5:13–15)

The Bible tells us to put others' interests before our own, but in our Americanized lives, what does that look like? My parents are a great example of people who show compassion in relationships. Ever since I was young, they helped other people by inviting them into their lives. Growing up, I experienced many different people living with our family at various times as a result of my parents helping them out. We shared our Christmases with people who were suffering in one way or another. We served at the homeless shelter for Thanksgiving a few times. As long as I can remember, my parents have been willing to help others even if it interrupted their own plans.

They had this approach with others because they had a firm understanding that the purpose of their lives was to serve Jesus and help others. When you grasp the biblical perspective that all people have value and worth, and when you know that your calling as a believer in Christ is to be His hands and His feet (1 Corinthians 12:12), then it is easier to have compassion for others and think of others' needs above your own.

Sometimes we behave selflessly or compassionately but for the wrong reasons. When we help others in an effort to be accepted or to *look* like a good friend, then our motives are selfish rather than selfless. Examine your heart and adopt a Christlike perspective, valuing others above yourself. Ultimately, an examination of your heart and an adoption of Christ's selfless compassion toward others will improve both your experience of other people and their experience of you. Next time someone irritates you, consider asking God to help you shift your perspective of the person and the situation, and watch as His grace transforms the moment.

Fear of Rejection

Past relationships affect how we see current relationships. Sometimes we struggle with relationships for fear of rejection. When I was growing up, I was different from other girls. I was not really into the things that other girls were into. I have a slightly rare personality type. A popular personaliy test has shown that in my most natural state, I am task focused and introverted socially. I am not a people pleaser. Even though I care about other people very much, I often forget to ask how they are doing because I am so focused on the task at hand. I think that is why God called me to be a therapist. When therapy is the task, I can relate to people in a way that does not come naturally to me in other settings.

When I was young, I got along with guys better than girls because of my personality. I did not like all the drama that came with relationships with other girls. In high school, most of my close friends were guys. This left me super lonely during holiday breaks because I didn't play video games like most of my guy friends did. I spent a lot of time hanging out at my guy friends' houses talking to their moms while my friends played their newest video games.

It seemed like the other girls experienced me as cold or unfriendly. It felt like they would do whatever they could to take me down. I experienced all kinds of rejection from peers growing up. The pain and rejection that I experienced ran the gamut. Though I've blocked a lot of instances from my memory, I have many vivid memories of experiencing rejection including: being the only kid not invited to the birthday party at age 8, being told I was worthless and fat at age 10, being left out from girls' nights at age 11, being laughed at when I liked a boy and being told that no boy would ever like me at age 12, being given written letters of rejection from supposed friends at age 14, being rejected by the boy I liked after he made me think he liked me at age 15, being told by my close guy friends that they were not allowed to be my friend anymore per their girlfriends' requests at age 16, being called dirty words in the school hallways and bullied online by a friend's controlling boyfriend who wanted me out of her life at age 17, being told by other Christians that my heart was evil at age 18, and being told by the young man I was pining after that he wasn't interested in a romantic relationship at age 19.

As you can imagine, I formed emotional calluses over the years, otherwise I don't think I would have survived it all. Some of those times I could feel God with me, but many of those times I just felt alone. People often told me that I had a lot to offer and the fact that boys saw me more as a friend than a girlfriend was God's protection over me, but it never felt that way. I was often told that the girls were jealous of me and I had a lot of good qualities. Again, those attempts at encouragement fell on deaf ears. Looking back, I do not know if the words intended to comfort me were true, but what I do know is that God was allowing me to experience all that rejection for a bigger purpose.

I finally started to heal from the depths of these painful experiences the year before I met my husband, Mike. I felt God calling me to stop looking for a husband and to set my eyes on Him. Jesus used that time to help me work through my fear of rejection. It is a good thing too. If I had brought all that baggage into our marriage and then we had to face the trials we faced, it would have been a nightmare. God brought me on a journey, and through all of that rejection, I learned two things about relationships. 1) We cannot have healthy relationships with others if we do not have a healthy relationship with Christ. 2) Our relationships with others do not define who we are; only our relationship with God can define us. (See Chapter 3 for a refresher on how God defines you.)

Accepted By Jesus

Although you have experienced rejection in past relationships, you will not experience rejection from Jesus Christ. If rejection from your past has hindered your ability to have peace about your salvation, I want to encourage you that Jesus understands your rejection. He will never reject you as a believer. You have a bigger purpose in your life, and that is why it so often seems like the world rejects you. Do not live your life afraid of rejection. Deepen your relationships with other believers, and this will strengthen you. If your current Christian relationships are not able to support you and encourage you to grow in Christ, then you might need to find other Christian relationships too.

> As you come to him, the living Stone—rejected by humans but chosen by God and precious to him— you also, like living stones, are being built into a spiritual house to be a holy priesthood, offering spiritual sacrifices acceptable to God through Jesus Christ.
>
> (1 Peter 2:4–5)

> Greater love has no one than this: to lay down one's life for one's friends. You are my friends if you do what I command. I no longer call you servants, because a servant does not know his master's business. Instead, I have called you friends, for everything that I learned from my Father I have made known to you. You did not choose me, but I chose you and appointed you so that you might go and bear fruit—fruit that will last—and so that whatever you ask in my name the Father will give you. This is my command: Love each other. "If the world hates you, keep in mind that it hated me first. If you belonged to the world, it would love you as its own. As it is, you do not belong to the world, but I have chosen you out of the world. That is why the world hates you.
>
> (John 15:13–19)

> Walk with the wise and become wise, for a companion of fools suffers harm.
>
> (Proverbs 13:20)

As iron sharpens iron, so one person sharpens another.

(Proverbs 27:17)

Negative Thinking of Others

How we see other people affects how we relate to them. Our relationships struggle if our perspective is off. When we are judgmental, assume what others' intentions are, fear rejection, or forget to invite Jesus into our relationships, our relationships will suffer. The way we think about people affects our relationships with them even when we try not to let it.

There have been many times in managing our business that others have criticized either the business or me, and that negativity has affected my relationship with them. Not only does it affect how they see me, it also affects how I see them.

With my personality, I grew up feeling like I needed to protect myself by disconnecting from people who didn't like me. As a business owner and manager, I cannot do that. I have to rise above the criticism and negativity in order to maintain professionalism.

This has been a learning experience for me. I have had to process the relationships from my past that shaped my perspective, and I have had to take a hard look at the ways that I learned to protect myself by pulling away from others. I have learned that by sticking it out, even when I have experienced criticism or rejection, the relationship can still be positive. There can be positive things on the other side of the criticism where the relationship can grow. I never would have known this if God hadn't led me to showing my heart in the face of criticism instead of running away.

- Do you think negatively about others when something does not go your way?

- How does hearing others' negative opinions affect how you think about them?
- Do you push people away when negativity arises in your relationships?
- How can you rise above the negativity in order to keep strong relationships with those people God has put in your life?

Not only do we sometimes think negative things about others but we often assume the worst of their intentions. Being a business owner I am so offended when clients or staff assume that we made a decision for selfish reasons when in reality we carry a heavy burden to care for our clients and staff. When I start to experience disappointment in what others think of me, God reminds me that I can make similar assumptions of others. I can be just as guilty of assuming that someone else has selfish intentions when their action or decision impacts me negatively and I don't know the whole story or I am just assuming I know what they think.

One small example of this comes up often in a typical marriage. Maybe the wife likes a cleaner kitchen than what the husband prefers. Maybe the husband knows this, and he tries to keep the kitchen clean. But because his standard for a clean kitchen is lower than his wife's, it's easy for him to overlook a level of cleanliness that his wife prefers. The wife might assume that her husband is being selfish and would rather watch TV instead of helping out. But maybe the husband just didn't notice the things that the wife noticed. Had he noticed, he would have gladly helped to better clean the kitchen.

- How often do we do this with others?
- Do you assume you know what others' intentions are?

- Do you think negatively about people and then pass it along through gossip or "venting"?

These habits can affect your relationships without you realizing their potential damage.

Anger Toward Others

Anger may be valid when our values have been violated, a boundary has been crossed, or trust has been broken; however, it can also be an immature or irrational reaction to a common situation such as not getting our way. Anger often affects our relationships. Our relationship with Jesus is the most important relationship in our lives. When life gets hard or when we have to deal with the sin of this world, we sometimes get angry with God. We might get mad at God for putting boundaries around us when we want to do something that is against God's Word. We sometimes carry little bits of anger toward God without even realizing it.

Many times throughout motherhood, I felt like God gave me a little nudge to remind me that the picture of my love for my kids is just a small portion of the picture of His love for us. When that happens, my understanding of the dynamics of God as the loving Father deepens. For instance, my two oldest kids are rambunctious and strong-willed. As babies, they would throw fits when I put them down or did something that they didn't like. However, my thirdborn has been much more laid-back and happy. Yet on a particular day, he was angry with me. Even at only 14 months old, he was really angry with me and I knew it.

He was tired. Mike tried to put him down for a nap, but after a few minutes of my son crying, I went into his room to try to calm him down. As I rocked him in his room, I realized that he was much too squirmy to settle down, so I gave up and brought him downstairs with me. I planned to try and put him back down for a nap after a little bit. That trick often worked with my daughter when she was little. It was like a reset to the routine, and it helped her to eventually get to sleep. So I brought my son downstairs, put him into his gated baby safe zone, and shut the gate behind me. As I did this, he started to throw a little fit. He knows that a closed gate means he doesn't get to roam freely around the house.

I told him that it was naptime so he could sit with me in the rocking chair. When I sat down with him, his fit grew louder. He did not want me to hold him. He wiggled his way out of my arms and onto the floor, continuing to cry and growl. He crawled into a corner to hide and made it clear he did not want me to draw close to him. After a minute, he was still not calming down, so I scooped him up and rocked him and sang. He just looked right at me and growled, quivering teeth and all. I continued to rock him, trying to calmly soothe him and he slowly calmed down.

As I rocked him I realized that just as my baby was mad at his momma, I too get mad at my heavenly Father sometimes. My son must get it from me because when I am angry or even just annoyed, I want to push others far away and be left alone. As I watched my precious little one work out his frustration, God brought clarity to my heart. Amidst his fits, I continued to love on him. What a great reminder of God's love for us. Even if you are mad at God because of a seemingly unbearable circumstance or pain that you have endured, God continues to love you just the same. Let God hold you in His arms even if you are growling at Him. Don't push Him away rather let God comfort you even when you are angry with Him. Harboring anger toward God will affect your relationship with

Him. He loves you, and He loves to comfort you. Let Him.

When I am angry at others, I push them away just as my son did with me. God used this example with my son to show me that I need not push Him or people away. The Bible calls us to show gratitude and forgive others.

> Be kind and compassionate to one another, forgiving each other, just as in Christ God forgave you.
>
> (Ephesians 4:32)

I felt convicted at that moment to let go of anger and pursue relationships that I had lost. Don't let a lack of gratitude or a lack of forgiveness cause anger in your heart toward others.

I also considered that if I feel others pushing me away, I need to do the same as I did with my son—I need to love them through it with compassion. You will strengthen your relationships when you can manage your anger, forgive others, show gratitude, and offer compassion. If others are angry with you, do not run from them or let them push you away. Lean into the relationship. In time, you will walk away with a stronger friendship.

- Do you get angry?
- What is the root of your anger?
- Are you angry with God?
- Does that anger affect your relationships?
- Do you push people away when you are mad?
- Do you allow your heart to lack gratitude and forgiveness?
- Do you push people away?

Some of us have a tendency to push people away when we should not. We don't like the pain of conflict so we give up on relationships. Do not let anger get in the way of your relationships.

In relationships that God has ordained, we are supposed to stay committed no matter how angry we are, how negatively we think about the relationship, or how little compassion we feel for them. However, you could have unhealthy boundaries with people who are bringing chaos or damage into your life, and in those times it is important to consider how to healthily distance yourself from harmful relationships.

> "You have heard that it was said, 'Love your neighbor and hate your enemy.' But I tell you, love your enemies and pray for those who persecute you,
>
> (Matthew 5:43–44)

Biblical Commitment

As a therapist, I walk many clients through figuring out a balance in their commitment to the people in their lives. Commitment to relationships and our understanding of God's plans for our relationships is the difference between success and failure with people. Relationships take two people in order for them to be healthy, but as all clients learn in counseling, we can only control our part of the relationship. There is clinical evidence in certain therapy models that has shown that, although you cannot control what the other person does, significant progress can be made in a relationship when only one person is committed to making changes to better the relationship.

There are times, however, in which one person can put in significant efforts but the negative dynamics of a relationship do not change. In these situations the Holy Spirit will guide you, if you seek Him, to determine the level of commitment that He is calling you to have with these certain people in your lives. Sometimes the level of commitment is suprising or changes over the years. Keeping your heart open to the leading of the Holy Spirit is important in staying healthy and balanced in relationships.

In counseling, some of our clients struggle to see which friendships or significant others might be bringing more negativity and stress into their lives rather than connection and companionship. I have also seen adults struggling to determine their level of emotional commitment to their parents once they have started their own family, especially if their relationship with their parents brings with it unhealthy levels of stress.

One of the most common relationships that brings people to counseling is the relationship of marriage, and often people approach counseling in hopes of better determining what level of commitment is healthiest within their struggling marriage. We typically advocate for saving the marriage, but in situations of abuse, addiction, or abandonment we understand things are more complicated. When it comes to a biblical opinion of ground for divorce, we always refer a client back to their pastor.

Many people enter marriage hoping for a fairytale in which they will live happily ever after. Before we were married, another Christian couple mentored Mike and I, and we took premarital classes through our church. Through this, we learned the biblical and eternal perspective that marriage is not designed to make you happy, and it is not supposed to be easy. Rather marriage exists for our sanctification. Marriage is supposed to rub off your rough edges and make you more like Christ. Mike and I learned that in order to have a successful marriage, we must have a healthy perspective about marriage. "Divorce is not an option" and "No matter what concerns we have, God has a purpose for this marriage so we cannot give up on it" are two helpful perspectives we have clung to over the years.

As is normal in some marriages, Mike and I are very different. But we are like oil-and-water kind of different. For example, it took us 14 years to find a hobby that both of us actually like to do together. We have spent many date nights just driving around because we can't decide what we would both like to do. (Of course, he doesn't mind to just drive around aimlessly even though it stresses me out.) We have different ideas about what diet is healthiest, how to keep the house clean, which projects should be done first (if we ever get to them), and what kind of work/life balance is healthiest just to name a few of our many differences. We have to compromise on almost every TV show or movie we watch because our preferences are so vastly different.

Our first few years of marriage were rough, as many young marriages are, but we were often fighting about the little insignificant things in addition to the usual big stuff. I can remember fighting about something so minor for so long that I started to literally hit my head against a wall (I guess that's where the expression comes from).

On top of that, Mike, struggled with intense anxiety and depression for a few years, and I genuinely did not know what our future might hold. I was worried that I would have a husband who was unable to function and might end up needing constant care. At times Satan tried to put thoughts in my head that marriage was too hard and I was too weak. During that dark season, the perspective that God has a plan for our marriage became my life raft.

Mike is an amazing husband and father, and through his own journey, he has received enormous blessing and healing from God. Mike is loving, supportive, smart, and helpful. He loves the Lord, and he has integrity. You will even get to hear from him later in this book when he shares more of his story during the chapter on depression. However, when we were young and some of our rough edges had not worn off yet, I was less patient, less compassionate, and less understanding than I have learned to be 14 years later. Mike was struggling with a real mental health problem and I was not patient, loving, or helpful like you might think I would be as a mental health therapist. Instead I was just mad a lot of the time, and I feared the responsibility of our family life might fall on me.

What a blessing it is that as I held onto the perspective "God has a purpose in our marriage." Mike was holding onto the perspective that "Divorce is not an option." If we hadn't had these perspectives, I would have sunk into my own depression and entertained thoughts that the grass is greener on the other side of the fence. Instead I pressed into God and searched for what He had for us to learn through that trying time.

I cried out to God in my pain, and I desperately pleaded for healing for Mike and strength for myself. The pain was so real that when God blessed us with a new home, I couldn't enjoy it. I would imagine myself busting up the walls with a sledgehammer because I harbored so much pain and anger. Staying focused on God's purpose in our marriage, even in the pain, gave me the strength to survive. I am certain that being able to focus on what God wants me to learn through our marriage struggles is what saved our marriage, and that same perspective will continue to save our marriage as we face new trials in life together.

Not everyone has our story. Some marriages have less conflict, while others are violent or damaging, and each person has to determine their level of commitment for themselves. But what I know about God's call on our lives is that He wants us to commit to our spouse, and He wants both spouses to turn to Him in hard times. In doing so, we allow the conflict to make each of us more like God Himself.

Relationships are hard because we are all broken and sinful people with different ways of looking at things. Marriage is by far the hardest relationship most of us will ever enter into, and it is the relationship that Satan most attacks because it is supposed to be a picture of Christ's relationship with the church. Thinking about it that way, if Satan can destroy your marriage then he has gained ground in your life. Be aware of Satan's attacks on your marriage.

If any of this seems unclear to you about how you should be committed in certain relationships, know this, our first commitment is to Christ. Once you put Christ first, then we are to seek Him in determining the boundaries we need to have in relationships with others. Second to our relationship with Christ, our most important relationship is marriage.

God's plan for marriage, under most circumstances in which everyone is safe and faithful, is that a marriage should remain unbroken in order to bring glory to God. If separation is needed, attempts to reconcile are to be made.

Maybe the relationship in which you are most struggling is with a life long friend or family member. Maybe that person struggles with addiction or a personality disorder, and the realities of being in a relationship with them may weigh heavily on you. For family and friends, the Bible says that you are to let your light shine to others, loving them as Christ does (Matthew 5:16). But the Bible also says to leave your family behind if that is necessary to you following Christ. So seek the Holy Spirit and He will guide you as to what level of commitments to have in each of your relationships.

Biblical Attitude

The last variable affecting your relationships that is on my heart to share is the value of having a biblical attitude. Your attitude is seen by others, even if you try to hide it. What we pass along to others matters. Other Christians and non-Christians are looking at you as an example of Jesus. Sometimes we will have a negative attitude and need to work it through. If you can embrace a biblical perspective on eternity, God, yourself, and others as we have discussed, this will affect your attitude.

I encourage you to go to Jesus to work out negative attitudes when they arise so as to not affect your relationships. You may think that venting to others about something has no harm, however, even if that venting remains confidential, a negative and grumbling attitude is almost always toxic.

I once worked with someone who was often trying to help other staff members. But once the news of the ways she was helping got to her superiors, it seemed as though it was actually not very helpful at all. It was actually passing along perspectives about the business that were making the staff culture toxic. When I heard her explain it, she seemed to have good intentions. However, when I stepped back and looked at the whole picture I saw a different story. I tried to ignore the situation in an effort to avoid drama, but the toxicity she was fueling became unavoidable, and myself and another coworker felt led to confront her about her attitude.

We have all been guilty of fueling toxicity in some capacity. I have done it for sure. The Bible warns us against grumbling and gossiping. We affect the people around us with our words. Even though I still struggle with these things, over the years I've improved. I grumble and gossip less.

While I still sometimes grumble and I'm certainly not an expert at refraining from complaining (you can ask my husband), I have learned to better refrain from these tempting habits. When I can keep my eyes fixed on the things above, and when I refresh my memory on the proper perspectives of things, I am more successful and much less likely to grumble, complain, and pass along a negative perspective.

In your relationships there are a number of questions to consider.

- Do you embrace compassion?
- Do you consider what others might be going through before you get offended?
- Do you seek ways to serve others?
- Do you fear rejection? Do you hide when things get tough?
- Do you think negatively of others?
- Do you assume other's intentions or struggle with anger?
- Are you committed to making your relationships work?
- How is your attitude?
- Do you grumble or gossip with others?
- Are you fueling negative perspectives or encouraging positive perspectives?

How you think affects your relationships, and your attitude affects others' attitudes. In Matthew 22 it states:

> Jesus replied: "'Love the Lord your God with all your heart and with all your soul and with all your mind.' This is the first and greatest commandment. And the second is like it: 'Love your neighbor as yourself.' All the Law and the Prophets hang on these two commandments."
>
> (Matthew 22:37–40)

When you allow these verses to serve as the cornerstone of your relationships, you will begin to experience a shift in your perspective of others that ultimately transforms your relationships.

CHAPTER 6

THE BATTLE FOR OUR PERSPECTIVE

As Christians, we are in a spiritual battle, and we have forces that are against us. The Bible tells us that Satan, or the devil, is against us. He uses our thoughts, circumstances, experiences, and other people (among other things) to work against us. He wants to distract us, and he wants us to be stuck in our emotions so that we are unable to think logically. His desire is for us to live in pain and suffering rather than live in peace and joy in the Lord, which is God's desire for us. As a therapist, I intently listen to a person's story to help him or her determine where they are stuck in the way they think about and process things. There is also a sinful flesh aspect and a biochemical element that can be present when someone is struggling with stress, fear, overthinking, anxiety, or depression.

Although it can prove invaluable, working with a therapist is not the only way to gain insight into these things. To identify where you are stuck and/or where you need to further grow and develop, it is crucial to spend time in prayer with God to best understand your unique battle. It is extremely important to have a proper understanding about the components that are waging war against us in order to most effectively fight both Satan and our own sinful flesh. Without a proper understanding of these forces, it is difficult to adequately challenge a distorted perspective or move healthily through trials and suffering.

Identifying Your Spiritual Battle

In Chapter One, I explained the concept of intrusive thoughts. Clients who are diagnosed with anxiety disorder often report having a significant amount of intrusive thoughts that affect their everyday functioning and well-being. As a Christian counselor I find it very interesting that secular psychology identifies these thoughts as meaningless. Secular psychology suggests that intrusive thoughts do not stem from our true selves rather they are a result of our brain playing tricks on us and are typically opposite from who we are at our core. Considering the perspective that we are in a spiritual battle and that Satan wants to devour us, it is obvious to me that intrusive thoughts may not always be some form of inner trickery. Rather intrusive thoughts may actually be lies that our enemy formulates in an effort to trap us into something that derails us from our proper perspective.

If we can identify that we are under spiritual opposition, whether it is from Satan or from our own sinfulness, we can address some of our core issues that are causing us to be stuck in an improper perspective. Understanding and identifying spiritual opposition allows us to confront a lie from Satan rather than letting it define ourselves. For clients who request Christian counseling, using this lens allows me to properly assess, diagnose, and set a course for treatment to heal the whole person, body, mind, and soul. If one doesn't realize that their problem stems from lies or sin, they might spend time, energy, and resources looking for solutions in all the wrong places.

Excessive drinking of alcohol, retail therapy, exercise, television, sleep, food, and other addictions and compulsions are all common ways that people cope with problems that ultimately can only be solved through a perspective change. Not only is it important that we learn how to change our thinking to be Christlike, it is also important that we learn how to maintain that Christlike perspective. While you may still struggle with the same old things over and over again (you will always be you, after all), you will be able to realign yourself with the Truth of Scripture much easier when you can identify and understand Satan's schemes.

Our Enemy's Schemes

Through the Scriptures, God reminds us to stay alert and be aware of Satan's schemes. When we allow Satan to stir up our thoughts, to persuade our fears, and to influence our hearts through his lies, we allow him to minimize God's lordship over our subconscious minds. When this happens it does more than just affect our beliefs. It also begins to taint our filter for interpreting all of life. We have to pay attention enough to recognize when our perspective is being influenced by Satan so that we can resist him.

Do you have an understanding of what it looks like when the devil is stirring your thoughts and persuading your fear? Can you see it happening? Scripture makes it clear that a spiritual realm does exist. Even so, most of us don't think about it much, and we live our days forgetting about its existence.

Do you realize that feelings such as discouragement, anger, defeat, and fear can often be a spiritual attack of Satan? It is important to understand that every day you are living in a spiritual battle. Satan attacks in a variety of ways. Feeding and fueling every negative thing in your life is just one way that Satan attacks, and he does so all day, every day.

Satan knows the power of your perspective. Do you? As the Bible tells us the following in 1 Peter:

> Be alert and of sober mind. Your enemy the devil prowls around like a roaring lion looking for someone to devour.
>
> (1 Peter 5:8)

What does that look like? How do you think Satan devours someone? He devours us through our minds, through our thoughts, and through our perspectives. Then, once our perspective has been compromised, our intentions, actions and behaviors will likely follow.

Think about the fear, anxiety, sinful anger, selfishness, or sin that is holding you back.

- What do you think about that sin?
- Do you know that it is something you should work to overcome but you keep failing to conquer?
- When you give into temptation, what are you thinking?
- What perspective do you have about it?
- Do your thoughts justify your actions?
- Do you tell yourself, "It's not that bad"? Or maybe you think that you won't ever be able to conquer it so why even try?
- Do you rationalize it with reasons such as, *I'm tired, I was treated unfairly, My hormones are out of whack* or, *I have biological needs*?

- Do you compare your sin to someone else's and think, *What I'm doing isn't as bad as that?*

This is how the devil devours us through our perspective.

With the right perspective, a perspective focused on the power of the Holy Spirit within us, we can stand strong against the evil one, stopping those temptations immediately and allowing God's strength to keep us from being devoured. That is the power of having a Christlike perspective.

Satan's Battle Plan

Satan's battle plan is to corrupt our minds in order to devour us, to lead us into self-destructive thinking, and to keep us doubting God's truth. He is crafty and deceptive. He challenges the authority of God's Word and disputes God's character. He manipulates us into thinking that God is asking us to miss out on important things in life. He promises pleasure and happiness in doing sinful things and thinking sinful thoughts. He is very strategic in his plans so as to draw us into his way of thinking.

Now the serpent was more crafty than any of the wild animals the Lord God had made. He said to the woman, "Did God really say, 'You must not eat from any tree in the garden'?" The woman said to the serpent, "We may eat fruit from the trees in the garden, but God did say, 'You must not eat fruit from the tree that is in the middle of the garden, and you must not touch it, or you will die.'" "You will not certainly die," the serpent said to the woman. "For God knows that when you eat from it your eyes will be opened, and you will be like God, knowing good and evil." When the woman saw that the fruit of the tree was good for food and pleasing to the eye, and also desirable for gaining wisdom, she took some and ate it. She also gave some to her husband, who was with her, and he ate it.

(Genesis 3:1–6)

In the book of Genesis when Satan tempts Eve, he acts like he is looking out for her best interest and then he attempts to weaken her identity. He questioned God's love for her. He said something like, "If God loved you, He wouldn't keep you from something." Eve began to doubt God's lordship, God's love, and God's words. And then Satan pounced, straight-out contradicting God. Satan told Eve she wouldn't die. Satan's lie grew deeper, and he promised Eve that she would be "like God" if she ate the forbidden fruit. Eve began to see the tree differently.

Her perspective was changing, and her flesh began to take over. She saw that the tree was "good for food and pleasing to the eye, and also desirable for gaining wisdom…." Satan had her stirred up, so-to-speak. Eve wasn't even thinking about the tree prior to this conversation with Satan, but after, Eve was analyzing the tree. She was experiencing lust of the eye, lust of the flesh, and a desire to be like God (which is pride). Sadly, we sometimes fall into a similar trap of temptation, often in a similar order.

When was the last time the Enemy stirred you up? The devil uses this same battle plan with us. If you can recognize it and hold onto God's truth from the beginning, then you can stand your ground and use the power of the Holy Spirit to ensure victory over the evil one. Before Eve even considered taking a bite of the forbidden fruit, she made a fatal mistake: She allowed Satan to engage her thoughts. Satan is cunning, and he baited her. She took the bait, and as a result she began to analyze her situation. She began to consider what she was missing, how things could be better, and what more she could get out of life if only she had something that she didn't currently have.

Satan got his hooks in her the moment they engaged in conversation, and he began to lure her into his way of thinking. This is exactly what happens to us as well. Satan starts by planting seeds of doubt and discontentment, and before we know it, we question our situation, wondering if it could be better. We begin to focus on the area of our lives that seems just out of reach for us, and we start to feel discontentment. Soon that discontentment turns into unhappiness, frustration, and anger with others, ourselves, and God. This is when Satan starts to gain ground in the battle.

When Satan Attacks

I have had times when I could sense that Satan was attacking me. In those moments, my thoughts and feelings were not my normal thoughts and feelings. I have also had times when it seemed like I was carrying two contradictory trains of thought. It is as if part of me realized that my anger or frustration was getting out of hand but another part of me wanted to focus on what was upsetting me. For me, when Satan attacks, it feels like I have two trains of thought that are traveling in opposite directions, both fighting for my attention. Whether or not this is an attack from Satan or simply a manifestation of my sinful nature is not so much the point. Even Satan is cunning enough to manipulate my sinful nature to work for his advantage, often fueling the battle with both lies and confusion.

Some of the hardest battles are when I allow Satan just enough room to get me started, and then I take over, building on what he began. A shallow roar from Satan that says "you aren't good enough" can quickly turn into a laundry list of things I don't like about myself. The list grows and grows as I stretch back into childhood, finding more and more to add to the pile. Sometimes there are even things that come up in those moments that I thought I had resolved. One of Satan's most powerful attacks targets us directly at the heart of our identity. He twists things so we start to define ourselves in a way that is misaligned with God's truth. It is in those moments when it is important for me to seek help and resources to better understand and overcome the battle waging war on my life.

One personal example happened when I faced a situation with a friend that triggered old thoughts of feeling inadequate and worthless. Satan had me questioning my identity and my worth. That trigger opened up a flood of memories of rejection, and bubbling up inside of me were familiar thoughts that something was wrong with my personality and that others do not care about me. I soon found myself wanting to isolate from others in an attempt to stop the spiral of memories and darkness.

I used to default to isolating myself because I have always felt different from other people. However, God has helped me to see that the ways in which I am different have wonderful purpose. As I shared in Chapters 1 and 5, I am an extrovert in relation to tasks, but I am an introvert in relation to other people. This has proved valuable in building our business; however, I can be viewed as unfriendly, too serious, and bossy. As you can imagine, my childhood was filled with a lot of rejection from other children because

I made people feel that way. The rejection I felt was worsened by Satan's lies that I then used to define myself.

So in this triggering situation, the lies that I believed during my childhood began to resurface. I tried to ignore them and reconnect with the healing work God had previously done in my life, but I was struggling. This situation rattled me, and I lacked a confident stance against the attacks. Instead of knowing that my thoughts and feelings were not my own, but rather an attack from the Enemy, I froze. Typically, I was able to have peace during similar battles by standing firm in my identity in Christ, but something about this situation was different. I cried every day. For two weeks, I was depressed and lethargic, and I struggled to function—so much so that I considered looking into taking antidepressant medications (which I had taken in the past). I believed there was something wrong with me, just as I had as a teenager. My husband urged me to start counseling again, and thankfully I did. My Christian counselor helped me to push through these new feelings and find healing in Jesus' truth once again.

Sometimes, something that we thought we had overcome resurfaces during a different season of life. We think that Satan can no longer bother us in that area, but instead we learn that new life seasons and experiences reveal the dusty, dark corners of an issue that still needs light and healing.

Healing for the Dark Corners

In working with clients, when we meet our current goals, I begin to help them plan for their future. I try to help them understand that there will be dusty and dark corners that still need illuminated, so that they are more prepared to deal with them should their next life season cause them to surface. Clients who have experienced the death of a spouse or a child may have deeper emotions that surface if they remarry or have another child. Clients who have unhealthy or tense relationships with their parents may need to work through dark corners that become illuminated once they become parents themselves. Clients who have expereinced sexual abuse may have pain that's still hiding, waiting to resurface at a later time. As a therapist I know the importance of dealing with the pain whether it is in preparing for a future marriage, a future family, or the future resurfacing trauma. It is perfectly normal to need support again as you work through the pain and fight against the lies that Satan is once again whispering in your ear.

In these times, Satan wants us to get stuck again so that our growth is stunted and we gravitate toward a self-destructive path. He wants us to feel puzzled as to why this struggle is resurfacing. Don't let Satan have any ground in this. One strategy against Satan's schemes is to seek help in identifying these dark corners in order to work through the healing process. It is important to know the life situations that may bring further light on past pain. It helps to approach the next situation or season of life more prepared so that we can best deal with resurfacing pain, anxiety, or trauma.

I found that when God delivers healing into spaces that we thought we had figured out, the healing permeates a greater depth of our hearts and souls. So in my triggering situation, instead of beating myself up about this resurfaced issue and getting stuck in the pain and depression, I embraced the process as I met with my counselor. This is when I experienced for myself that healing can come in layers, and fighting Satan's lies echoing in our minds is a continual battle. Through this understanding, I was able to develop a stronger grasp on the truth of how God defines me.

Sometimes new situations or a life change such as marriage, kids, a new job, or even trauma gives opportunity for a richer experience of healing. The new situation opens a new layer of emotional baggage from our childhood, and we are able to work through it again with new insights. We can redefine our definition of self as we embrace God's truth on a deeper level.

Do you ever wonder why something you thought you had overcome has returned or resurfaced? Don't be discouraged. You're still making progress. It could just be a dark corner or new layer coming to light, and as you work through it again, God will bring you to a deeper level of healing. Trust God knowing that if the issue comes up again, you will be able to stand stronger against it the second, third, and fourth time around. The Holy Spirit will strengthen you in your battle against our enemy. The more you learn how to fight Satan's attacks, the quicker he will flee. Be alert, and catch him before you get stuck in the downward spiral of his lies and self-destructive thoughts that can give Satan ground in his attempts to devour us. The Bible tells us about what we can use against Satan's schemes. We can put on spiritual armour and have a battle plan of our own.

Our Armor

If this concept of spiritual battle is overwhelming be encouraged because the Bible gives us a great strategy for fighting off spiritual attack. Maybe you have found yourself in an ongoing battle but you haven't found freedom yet. Maybe your struggle is not with the dark corners or the new layers but rather you feel like Satan has full victory over certain issues in your life. Maybe you haven't surrendered any aspect of that issue to Christ for healing. In Ephesians 6 we are told to:

> Put on the full armor of God, so that you can take your stand against the devil's schemes. For our struggle is not against flesh and blood, but against the rulers, against the authorities, against the powers of this dark world and against the spiritual forces of evil in the heavenly realms. Therefore put on the full armor of God, so that when the day of evil comes, you may be able to stand your ground, and after you have done everything, to stand. Stand firm then, with the belt of truth buckled around your waist, with the breastplate of righteousness in place, and with your feet fitted with the readiness that comes from the gospel of peace. In addition to all this, take up the shield of faith, with which you can extinguish all the flaming arrows of the evil one. Take the helmet of salvation and the sword of the Spirit, which is the word of God.
>
> (Ephesians 6:11–17)

The metaphor of armor was significant for the original audience of these verses, and it is significant for us still today. This passage gives the picture of a soldier getting ready for battle, a battle in which we are fighting daily, even if we are not aware of it. We are to wear a belt of truth. Roman soldiers wore large heavy belts, kind of like a weightlifter's belt. All the other pieces of armor connected to the belt to ensure that it stayed in place and did it's job to protect the soldier.

God tells us to stand firm with the belt of truth buckled around our waists. It seems logical that truth is what is needed to ensure all the pieces of armor are being held together before we go into battle. Scripture memorization is a great way to strengthen your belt of truth. Find a verse that speaks to your most frequent attack. The belt is what held the breastplate in place for Roman soldiers.

Once you are clear on biblical truth, your identity will also be clear. The breastplate is what identified soldiers from one another and protected their major organs (i.e. lungs, heart, stomach). We are to have a breastplate of righteousness. This breastplate of righteousness identifies us as children of God and protects us from the troubles of this fallen world. It is crucial to have a firm grasp on God's truths in order for our armor to be secure. Our perspective aligns our righteousness, our thoughts, and our actions. If we do not understand God's truth, it is easier to act according to our flesh. We must protect ourselves with Christ's righteousness so that we will not be vulnerable to attacks from the Enemy. Doing so will give us confidence in who we are in Christ so we can stand steady against Satan's attacks on our identity.

God encourages us to have our "feet fitted with the readiness that comes from the gospel of peace." Knowing salvation in Jesus and focusing on His return provides our souls with peace and gives us the confidence we need to run into battle, and that peace provides us with stamina. We must have a firm grip of the gospel and the peace that it brings to successfully fight off the Enemy and the troubles of this world.

Your shield is your faith. Your faith, and your ability to have confidence in your faith, is your strongest defense. Your shield "can extinguish all the flaming arrows of the evil one." The shield is the first line of defense, and it protects you and the rest of your armor. Just as in a combat situation, your shield is to be used with purpose, strategy and awareness for it to have the most impact. Your shield can protect you. Matthew 6:13 tells us to pray against the attacks of the evil one on behalf of other believers. Paul tells us that all Christians are to use the tools given by God to fight off Satan when he attacks. So pray against the devil's attacks, and pray for others that they will grasp the truth, have faith in Jesus, embrace the peace of the gospel, and have a Christlike perspective. This will allow you and others to put on the armor of God and stand firm against our enemy.

We are to also put on the helmet of Salvation and take "the sword of the Spirit, which is the word of God." The helmet protects your head, and I don't think I have to explain how important it is to have a helmet in battle. Salvation in Christ is an important protection against Satan. As Romans 8:37–39 explains, nothing can separate us from the love of Christ. That includes Satan's attacks.

Finally we have our sword. As believers we have the sword of the Spirit, the only offensive weapon discussed in this chapter, as our offensive weapon. The Holy Spirit gives power to the Word of God. In order to use the sword efficiently in battle, we need to welcome, memorize, meditate on, and mobilize the Word of God. To mobilize the Word in battle, pray the Word, share the Word, and never stop reminding yourself of the Word of God. Just as Jesus did in Matthew 4:1–11, use Scripture to fight off Satan's temptations and attacks. Use Scripture to keep your perspective aligned with God's truth. If your use of the sword is not aligned correctly you won't be able to aim at your enemy with the intended full force of that weapon. Spending time in Scripture will continually strengthen all the pieces of your armour.

Our Battle Plan

Once we have on our armor, we can initiate our battle plan to fight back. Satan attacks us all the time, but as I see it, we have three advantages. 1) We have Jesus on our side who has overcome the world and conquered death, and we have the power of prayer. 2) We have the ability to discern God's leading through the power of the Holy Spirit. 3) We have the insight that the Enemy's goal is to devour us, and that he uses our minds to do so, leaving us ready to fight back.

Friend, I want to encourage you. Pray when things are going well, and pray when things are hard. Surrender your will and your plans so you can exchange them with God's will and God's plans. Pray that God would use you to further His kingdom, and pray against spiritual attacks that are happening all around you. Use your time in prayer to learn how to discern the Lord's direction in the still quiet moments and in the midst of the chaos. Pay attention to God's direction in the midst of Satan's lies or when negative thoughts are triggered. God will be there reminding your heart of His truth if you look for Him. Be clear minded and alert so you can pray and discern the Lord's direction for your life.

Knowing Satan's goal can help us identify his schemes. He may attack harder when we are taking steps in the right direction. He also attacks anything that God ordains for good. He hates it when we are trying to be a more loving spouse, more attentive parent, more diligent employee, more gracious friend, or more devoted follower of Jesus. He despises it when we are working toward a God-given goal such as starting a ministry, volunteering at church, becoming freinds with a neighbor, purifying our marriage, or working on something that will bring glory to God. In these times especially, we need to keep our eyes open to make sure that we are not allowing Satan to gain ground in the battle. We must remain aware of how he seeks to stunt our spiritual growth and intercept God's glory so we can avoid his efforts.

> Submit yourselves, then, to God. Resist the devil, and he will flee from you.
>
> (James 4:7)

The good news here is that Satan's attacks will not last forever. Satan and his demons are not able to be everywhere all the time. When we are being tempted by something or attacked in some way, we have been told what to do. If we can hold onto that truth and resist the path down which the Enemy is trying to lead us in our thoughts, Satan will flee from us.

I have noticed this many times in my own life. Sometimes Satan pushes the same buttons over and over because he knows that I struggle to control my reaction. I will notice very negative or disturbing intrusive thoughts in my head, and when I take them captive and submit them to the truth, they go away. It takes practice to take your thoughts captive, but we are not subject to the random negative thoughts we have or even the negative thoughts that seem to have evidence behind them. When Satan tries to put thoughts in our heads that cause us to start down a negative, critical, or sinfully angry path with ourselves or others, we can stand firm against them and resist the inevitable emotional rollercoaster. If you can do this, Satan will flee. It will not always feel so hard. Keep fighting and praying that you will gain understanding from each and every trial. God will deliver you from the attack in His timing.

- What buttons of yours does Satan like to push?
- What negative thoughts do you have that roll over and over in your head?
- What situations trigger you to beat yourself up?
- How do you fight back when Satan is attacking you?
- Do you have on your armour?
- Is your head protected with salvation?
- Is your belt strong with truth? Is your identity clear to you and others?
- Is your shield of faith strengthened with a biblical perspective so it can protect you?
- Is your sword of the Spirit mobilized?
- What Bible verses have you memorized that can speak to your heart in times of attack from the Enemy?
- How have you seen God deliver you from the Enemy's attack?
- What can you do differently in your thinking to stand against Satan's plan to devour you?

Friend, I want to encourage you to take a step back and look to see where the Enemy might be attacking you. When you are being attacked by feeling stressed, anxious, depressed, moody, angry, or just not yourself, fight back. Discern God's direction and hold tight to your shield of faith, your breastplate of righteousness, and your feet fitted with readiness. Do the work now to straighten your perspective so you will have a sturdy belt of truth. Fighting back is not easy at first, but sometimes a friend or spouse can help you have perspective on these attacks. Once you know how you are being attacked and what Satan's goal might be, fight back and regain your Christ-centered perspective.

CHAPTER 7
OUR PERSONAL PERSPECTIVE PROBLEM

In addition to Satan's opposition, we also have our own sinful beliefs and thoughts that are against us that can lead us into temptation and negativity. At times, it is hard to decipher the difference between all of the opposition that are working against us. Satan is the opponent in our spiritual battle, but there is another aspect of opposition that we encounter daily—our own sinfulness.

Sin makes it hard to have a Christlike perspective. We can be our own enemy when it comes to our thinking. Our sin opposes us when we have desires outside of God's will such as the desire to please man over God or a desire for wealth and success at all costs. It opposes us when we have a desire to justify unhealthy habits or look better than others. When we measure others against ourselves (and vice versa), we fuel an impossible standard that breeds competition, insecurity, and an insatiable need to feel good about ourselves. This is all sin, and it can cause problems in the way we think, behave, and perceive life. Reading Scripture, listening to biblical teaching, and prayer are three helpful tools to straighten out your thinking skewed by sin.

What is Sin?

The Bible is clear on sin. Sin is anything that falls short of God's standards. Sometimes this is unintentional and sometimes this is intentional. We are born with a sinful nature that opposes obedience to God. When sin is intentional, it is often because sinning is easier or appears more exciting than obedience. This is why we need Jesus to pay the penalty for our sin. Because of Him, our debt is paid, and even though we fall short of God's perfection, we can still enjoy heaven and eternity with Him.

If you have accepted Jesus's free gift of salvation, you are now credited Jesus' perfection in the sight of the Lord. Although we are credited His perfection, we still live with a sinful nature and must continue to choose to obey God. (Galatians 6:9, James 4:17, Romans 7:15–18, Matthew 26:41, Colossians 3:5–6, Romans 6:23, 2 Corinthians 5:21)

This concept can be difficult for many young or new believers. It is easy to learn these truths and think, *Because Jesus paid for my sin then why should I stop doing sinful things?* Examples of this might be drunkenness, sex outside of marriage, gossiping, grumbling, idolatry, lying, or cheating. It is easier to sin than to obey when the temptation feels too great, and knowing it is already forgiven makes it easy to justify.

Sometimes when considering sinfulness, Satan wants us to see God's law and commands as rules that are too strict. Friend, I want to propose a perspective on this that may help in those times when it seems that sin is inevitable. Just as a parent gives children rules to keep them safe and help them learn, God does the same for His children. Yes, you are forgiven but wouldn't you want to do the thing that the all-knowing God says is in your best interest?

I tell my kids to eat their vegetables because I know that it will make their bodies healthier. I tell my kids to be nice to each other to make their sibling relationship better. I tell my kids to forgive their bullies to make their hearts healthier. Similarly God instructs us to save sexual acts for marriage, not to drink to the point of intoxication, and to to be kind to others because obeying these commands will make our hearts, our bodies, and our relationships healthier. He also tells us not to sin. Unrepentant sin in our lives is unhealthy. Sin is a slippery slope toward significant spiritual suffering. I encourage you to strive to follow God's commands not out of a desire to be perfect or out of fear of doing something wrong, but rather strive to follow God's commands because in doing so you will develop, sustain, or grow healthier relationships and a healthier body, soul, and mind.

Can you look at God as a loving Father who is motivated to take care of you and guide you toward the healthiest and happiest life instead of seeing him as a tyrant? Do you see your sin as a bad habit that you need to work on, or are you okay with your sin because it's mild in comparison to what you deem really bad or awful? Everyone has to make their own decisions, but take a minute and ask God to show you what you need to surrender for the health of your heart, soul, relationships, and body.

Our Sinful Flesh

As Christians we likely know that we are human beings with the Holy Spirit living inside of us, but it is easy to forget how important these truths are to our daily lives. When we take this truth for granted, we are less capable of laying down our sinful flesh on a daily basis as is necessary to experience God's fullness for us. We know we are not perfect, but we aren't always aware of our own actions or which perspectives are trained by sin. It is so much easier to recognize sin in someone else.

We all know Christians who have blatantly sinful lives. We even know Christians whose sin is seemingly hidden. Likely you know of many Christians who have sinful patterns that are deeply affecting their lives. Maybe their sexual lust is complicating their relationships. Maybe their pride often leads to poor decisions. Maybe their materialism compromises a healthy balance in their life. Maybe this person is you. Likely you don't see how you are being impacted by such sin.

Sometimes the sins of others affect you personally. Maybe someone is continually critical or pushy toward you, or maybe someone is failing to offer you grace where you most need it. It is easy to wonder how they could see things so differently from you when you both follow the same God. It is easy to judge a friend who never seems grateful for the ways you help them or never returns favors or remains judgmental of others. We wonder how this person can be this way.

> This only have I found: God created mankind upright, but they have gone in search of many schemes."
>
> (Ecclesiastes 7:29)

> You hypocrite, first take the plank out of your own eye, and then you will see clearly to remove the speck from your brother's eye.
>
> (Matthew 7:5)

Scripture reminds us that we are all sinners, and our focus is not to be on the sin of others, rather it is to be on our own sinful nature.

Sometimes our sin issue seems to be too complicated or intricately tangled, and we can't imagine how to tackle it. We can become tempted to just accept it and no longer strive for freedom. Romans 6:6 tells us that when we are saved we are no longer slaves to sin. Then Romans 8:7–8 explains that we have a sinful nature that resists God. That sinful nature—our flesh—is part of our human experience. However, if we are saved by Jesus, we are no longer slaves to that flesh; we are no longer slaves to the sin in our lives. We actually become slaves of righteousness, although we still choose to sin at times (hence the battle).

Because we remain in our flesh, even as saved spiritual beings, the battle continues on and on and on, just as it did for the Apostle Paul in the book of Romans.

> I do not understand what I do. For what I want to do I do not do, but what I hate I do. And if I do what I do not want to do, I agree that the law is good. As it is, it is no longer I myself who do it, but it is sin living in me. For I know that good itself does not dwell in me, that is, in my sinful nature. For I have the desire to do what is good, but I cannot carry it out. For I do not do the good I want to do, but the evil I do not want to do—this I keep on doing. Now if I do what I do not want to do, it is no longer I who do it, but it is sin living in me that does it.
>
> (Romans 7:15–20)

Just like Paul, we have to battle our flesh, humble ourselves, and surrender hour after hour. We must continue to pray and seek God in order to overcome our flesh. Just as Jesus is always fighting for us (1 John 2:1–2), our flesh is always fighting against us (Galatians 5:17). I have had many people in my counseling office, while feeling defeated, say things such as, "Well I tried and God is not helping me" or "I prayed God would take this away but He has not." We have all felt that way. In those times we forget that our flesh does not want to surrender to God. Our flesh does not want to lay down the issue because in our humanity, we want to be in control. Friend, if you are feeling that way I encourage you to search your heart and identify areas in your life that may still need to be brought to submission to Christ. Only then will you start to find freedom in these sticky areas.

If we are not aware of our sinful flesh and our need to lay it down daily to follow Christ, we will remain stuck. The things of the flesh that cause destruction in our lives will continue to cause damage. These things can include our anger, judgment, depression, anxiety, obsessive tendencies, rigidity, disorganization, pridefulness, and dispersed attention. Interestingly, many of these things can also be diagnosed as mental health conditions if one does not consider their spiritual cause. Another therapist I work with has explained that in working with trauma survivors she sees anger, depression, and anxiety that comes from unhealed wounds (sins others have committed against us) and our own sinful reactions to cope with those wounds.

It is important to understand the role that our sinful flesh plays in our thoughts and in our mental health because in understanding this we can better understand the hurdle sin plays in how we function. Without this understanding, you may end up treating a condition unnecessarily. If we ignore the spiritual condition of our fallen nature, we likely will draw conclusions that don't include the full picture.

My Hidden Sin of Judging

I have struggled with my weight for as long as I can remember. As a kid, I was chubby, and by 5th grade I was significantly overweight. I always felt less (or more) than everyone else. I felt like there was something wrong with me. Kids at the small private school I attended were all thin, so I stuck out like a sore thumb. I had some friends, and some kids were nice to me at times, but other kids treated me terribly. I remember one time I walked by a boy in my class, and he called me "worthless" and laughed. I also saw all these super thin women on TV, and I wanted to look like them. In my naïveté, I hated my body, and I hated myself.

After thinning out naturally once puberty hit, I felt better about my weight. However, I still had lingering thoughts and worries about my weight and appearance. I was still a little thicker than a lot of my female peers. So I carried this narrative in my head that I was always going to be big and that was that. I was bitter about the biological genes I received, and it didn't help that my younger sister was thin and cute. I buried all of this down just enough to be okay with myself. God had worked on me enough through the years that I learned to love myself no matter what (or so I thought), even if I didn't like my body very much. Nonetheless this was still an issue I battled even though I told myself I didn't. I did not realize that I was stuck in a secular, dysfunctional habit of sinful thinking.

After my second pregnancy, I struggled to lose the baby weight as easily as did after my first pregnancy. When my daughter (my second child) was 18 months old, I was still carrying 20 more pounds than my pre-pregnancy weight (according to the BMI chart, I was considered overweight even at my pre-pregnancy weight). I was carrying around this 20-pound burden.

A friend of mine suggested that I see a holistic doctor who treats her patients with nutrition and supplements. I saw her for about a year and learned a lot about food. I learned about the dangers of processed foods and the importance of vegetables, fruits, and whole grains. I learned about the chemicals in our foods and environment that keep the pounds packed right to our hips, gut, and upper thighs. I learned about the lack of availability of good, affordable, healthy food here in America with our food manufacturers focusing on taste (more sugar), efficiency, and convenience (more preservatives, chemicals, and estrogen-like compounds).

When I was learning all of these things, I started to realize that my thoughts about myself and other people in relation to weight were actually sinful thoughts. I was making a correlation between my worth and my weight. These thoughts had me stuck in a negative space, even though I didn't realize it. I had enough understanding about my worth in Christ that my weight struggle was hiding in a dark corner.

After many hours of food preparation and staying on my feet constantly, I did lose some weight. I was eating healthier and more active, and those changes were impacting my appearance and my energy. However, I still had a sin issue. I would see other women who were bigger than me and feel relieved that I was thinner than them. I was proud. Similarly, I would look at women who were thinner than me and get jealous. I was envious. I realized that I had been doing this sinful comparison game my whole life.

By learning about the lack of quality food available, I started to gain compassion for women who seemed to struggle with their weight as I had for so many years. Maybe they didn't know that the convenient and yummy food they were eating was affecting their health. Maybe they couldn't afford all the organic vegetables, or maybe they worked too many hours and didn't have adequate time to prepare healthy food at home. As my perspective began to shift, my sin began to dissipate.

Even after I lost some weight, I was still in the overweight category. Though I was learning to overcome my sinful thoughts, my weight was still triggering a feeling of being unworthy at times.

At one point, we took our kids to a water park, and I was surrounded by people in bathing suits. I sensed my brain trying to return to the sin of comparing. When I noticed what was happening, I tried to lean into compassion. In doing so, the Holy Spirit brought something to my attention. At that moment, I realized that all those years of being the fat kid taught me to measure people's worth based on their weight, and I was measuring my own worth that way too. Maybe it took root when I was young and my classmate called me "worthless," or maybe it was simply years and decades of always seeing thin women on TV. Regardless, I had been believing the lie that my worth and my weight were inextricably connected. Worse yet, this lie had been living in my subconscious for most of my life.

As the Holy Spirit worked on my heart, two Scriptures came to mind:

> You, therefore, have no excuse, you who pass judgment
> on someone else, for at whatever point you judge another,
> you are condemning yourself, because you who pass judg-
> ment do the same things.
>
> (Romans 2:1)

> "Do not judge, or you too will be judged. For in the same
> way you judge others, you will be judged, and with the
> measure you use, it will be measured to you.
>
> (Matthew 7:1–2)

Those Scriptures hit me hard. I realized why I was feeling so unhappy with my body even after losing weight and spending so many hours over the last year getting healthy. This is why I had a self-esteem issue and a confidence issue. I even remember looking in the mirror before a business meeting, focusing on my chubby cheeks and thinking, *They will not respect you as a leader when you can't even control your weight.* I had always thought it was only about me. I never realized the depths that my judgments were pro-jected onto others. But God convicted me that day at the water park; my sinful flesh was not just measuring me but measuring others as well.

The way we measure others is how we measure ourselves. I was stuck in a judgmental thought process, and honestly, I didn't even recognize it as being judgmental. I just thought I was dealing with the facts of life. I was overweight, and I wouldn't like my body unless I was skinny. But I was trapped because of my thoughts. This realization and conviction hit me hard. Sinfully, I had set an impossible bar by which I measured myself and others. If I could just change my perspective and measure people as God does—on their hearts and not their bodies—I myself, would also be freed from the same measures that I had created (1 Samuel 16:7).

As time went on, my thought process began to strengthen in this area, and more often than not, I was letting others and myself off the hook. But after a third pregnancy in which I gained more weight than I had with my first two pregnancies, I started struggling with this measure again. As soon as I was done nursing, God alerted me to a diet plan that worked for me. I wasn't going to try it but something in my spirit felt a pressure to do so. I did; however, I almost quit because I thought if I did get thinner I would always look back at old pictures and judge myself for being fat. This is how deep my self-condemnation and judgment was. I was able to see that this thought was not healthy and repented of my attitude.

As time went on, God empowered me to stick with it, and for the first time since I was 18 years old, I was back down to a healthy BMI. I will likely continue to struggle to stay at a healthy BMI; however, I learned another important lesson through my weight loss journey that time. I learned that food can be an idol when we use it to comfort ourselves when we are hurting, to bring us joy that the Lord should bring, or to feel less stressed when we should be surrendering our fears to the Lord. I have learned to allow the truths of the Bible to be my comfort, my joy, and my rest instead of food, and that practice is part of my plan for remaining healthy physically, emotionally, and spiritually.

However, even now at a "healthy" weight (according to whoever decides what's healthy), I have times when I look in the mirror and don't like what I see. I see the love handles or the stretched out baby pouch, and I have to remember that I am in control of the standard by which I measure myself and others. I need to measure myself and others by the heart and not by the outward appearance. Through my weight loss journeys, I have learned the power of our sinful nature, and for me, I have to fight it daily. I need to fight my flesh that defaults to comparisons and judgments. If we are judgmental of others, then we are also using that same measure to judge ourselves. In doing so we end up trapped and unhappy.

Friend, I want to encourage you to strive to keep a biblical perspective daily so that you do not get sucked back into fleshly perspectives that hold you and others captive. Your battle might not be with your weight. It may be with how successful you are at work, how clean your house is, how well your kids are at sports, how much money you have, or how many friends like your social media posts. Whatever your earthly measure is, surrender it to Christ. Stop judging others so you can stop judging yourself.

Our Hidden Strongholds

> For though we live in the world, we do not wage war as the world does. The weapons we fight with are not the weapons of the world. On the contrary, they have divine power to demolish strongholds. We demolish arguments and every pretension that sets itself up against the knowledge of God, and we take captive every thought to make it obedient to Christ.
>
> (2 Corinthians 10:3–5)

Just as there are layers to our pain, there are also layers to our sin. Additional layers to our sinful flesh that run even deeper are hidden strongholds. A stronghold can be defined as a strongly defended belief; a physical stronghold can literally be a prison. In our negative strongholds, we are held prisoner to lies we believe or things that have been spoken over us. We become prisoners to a wrong way of thinking. Our strongholds are well defended from the truth to keep us captive to the lie. Sadly, we are most often the ones guarding our own strongholds, keeping that lie locked away in our hearts. We keep away the light that has the power to illuminate the truth that would set us free because at some point we subconsciously believed that the lie or way of thinking would protect us from something such as further rejection, failure, or pain.

Strongholds are thoughts like, "This is just part of who I am," "I never win," "No one can be trusted," "Bad things always happen to me," "God will only be happy if I do more good things," "I am invisible," "I am worthless," "My feelings are invalid," "I am unlovable," or "People always take advantage of me." Maybe at one time these lies felt like the only way to interpret a situation you experienced, but now it has become a self-built prison keeping you from the joy and freedom of Christ.

If the problem in your perspective is caused by a hidden stronghold, it will keep your perspective stuck in negativity. Strongholds prove to be more difficult to battle because they are also blind spots deeply rooted in lies. Strongholds are lies we have allowed to define us and our perception of reality for some time, and these strongholds require an intentional battle strategy. If you are battling something in your life that does not seem to budge, it may be a hidden stronghold.

If you have an improper perspective that does not want to change even though you are trying to fight it, you may have to dig deeper and ask the Lord to reveal to you what stronghold is hidden within you.

Some strongholds stem from how we were parented or cared for during our developmental years. A hidden stronghold can be something a sibling or another child did or said to us that our young mind absorbed as concrete truth. It can be something that a friend, spouse, boss, or coworker said or did to us, and even in our adulthood, we subconsciously decided to let those words define who we are. It can be a situation that held us back from an opportunity to reach our potential or a mistake that left us with tremendous guilt. It is often a conclusion we came to as we tried to understand the negative things in our lives. It can be anything that keeps us emotionally crippled for many years. For these hidden strongholds, we must seek the Lord for insight and healing, and we may need the help of another person to help us discern God's guidance throughout the healing process.

The best place to start is to pray for rescue from your strongholds. God answers our prayers, even when the relief does not come as quickly as we hoped. Sometimes God brings supernatural healing that happens all at once, and other times healing happens slowly over time. Sometimes God uses human means to remedy our situation, such as help from a doctor, medication, supplements, nutrition, long-term counseling, or coaching. Sometimes God gives us strength to handle the condition until He heals us, or sometimes He enables us to persevere until the day we meet Him in heaven and experience complete healing. Sometimes God wants us to find healing sooner than we do. Often God is eagerly waiting for us to turn to Him, break free, and accept His embrace with open arms. Regardless, a hidden stronghold has the power to keep us stuck for longer than necessary. So in those times when you do all you know how to do and still do not get the healing you want, it may be because of the spiritual battle going on and the strongholds that you have not let go of yet.

I know some Christians believe that healing should happen instantaneously, especially from things like anxiety and depression. Most often we need help to encounter Jesus in a healing way. There is no shame in seeing a counselor or therapist for a short time or a long time, and working with a life coach or pastor or even asking your doctor for medications can be conducive steps within your healing journey. But proceed with caution because when the medical and mental health professionals we seek do not offer a Christian perspective, we miss out on the most crucial factor in our healing process—Jesus Himself.

When I encounter a negative perspective in my thinking that won't budge regardless of the strategies I use to fight it, I seek help. Over the course of my life, I have seen a few different therapists and Christian mentors in an effort to get the support that I needed at the time. In fact, there was a season in which I was prescribed anxiety medication for a time to help me work through physical anxiety symptoms accompanied by heavy negative thoughts and feelings. There is no shame in the professional medical tools that God has given us to better facilitate our healing.

- Do you have a struggle that is especially persistent?
- Do you struggle with guilt, shame, depression, anger, anxiety, or fear?
- Do you fight off discontentment, negative thoughts, judgmentalism, or perfectionism?
- Do you have a tendency for procrastination, sarcasm, im-

patience, lack of self-control, lack of love, or selfishness?

- What situations in your past have you decided to let define you and the world around you?
- What hidden strongholds might be contributing to your misaligned perspectives about God, yourself, and others?
- What lies have you locked away in your heart that are causing you to struggle?

These hidden strongholds make it hard to have a Christlike perspective.

Friend, If you can turn your heart in repentance and reject the sin in your life, God can do great things. We often feel stuck or hopeless when we are struggling to change, but God is bigger than our weaknesses and our sin. If you are struggling, it can help significantly to reach out to someone—someone who loves Jesus— and ask them to help you change your perspective and keep you accountable to biblical thinking. In doing so, you can stop wasting the trials you endure, and instead you can use them to bring glory to God.

CHAPTER 8

PERSPECTIVE TO ALLEVIATE FEAR

We are all familiar with fear. Even children know fear. My 1-year-old is afraid of a new babysitter, my 5-year-old is afraid to try a new vegetable and my 8-year-old is afraid to change schools. Fear is not something that we outgrow. Teens may fear rejection from peers, young adults may fear not finding a job, mothers may fear their child falling off the swing set, and fathers may fear a lack of ability to lead their family through a difficult situation. Fear is the emotion that comes up when we face apparent danger, a new circumstance, or a difficult situation. Fear differs from anxiety. Anxiety is an obsession over the anticipation of hypothetical danger in the future or an obsession about a difficult situation that may or may not present itself. We will further discuss anxiety in the next chapter, but for now let's focus on fear.

Have I not commanded you? Be strong and courageous. Do not be afraid; do not be discouraged, for the Lord your God will be with you wherever you go."

(Joshua 1:9)

> Peace I leave with you; my peace I give you. I do not give
> to you as the world gives. Do not let your hearts be trou-
> bled and do not be afraid.
>
> (John 14:27)

My Own Fear

Even though I had a good foundation on God's goodness and my heart believed that God would redeem any pain I might go through for His glory, I still struggled to let go of fear as I was adjusting to motherhood.

Most parents learn quickly that their primary role as a parent during those earliest years is to keep their children alive. Left to their own devices, children would starve, injure themselves, walk into oncoming traffic, or choke on the little things they put in their mouths. During those early years of parenting, Satan's attacks on me were constant. He was quick to remind me any time my kids were out of my sight that something bad could happen to them, and he reminded me every time my husband left the house that it could be the last time I saw him.

Although there is some benefit to remembering that any moment could be our last, obsessing over that thought did not serve me as a wife and mother. Thinking too much of the negative made it hard for me to leave my kids with a new babysitter or let them do anything I perceived as risky. At times, my fear certainly crossed over into anxiety when the danger I perceived was not actually a reality. Through time in prayer and intentionally remembering God would redeem any pain that I might endure, I was able to start letting go of the fear of things I perceived as risky. In time I became a less nervous mother.

Letting go of fear was a game changer in my life. I could finally feel less anxious about things that weren't a threat, and I began to better enjoy my life. The reality is that bad things sometimes happen, and at some time or another we will all suffer sickness or injury (not to mention, death is inevitable). Those really are the facts of life. But if you can plant in your heart the truth of God's love, providence, and eternal plan for all of us, it becomes easier to have a proper perspective on those facts and face them with confidence that God has a plan for your life.

> I sought the Lord, and he answered me; he delivered me from all my fears.
>
> (Psalm 34:4)

Fear Can Turn into Anxiety

As a child, I only had one grandparent with whom I was close. My father's mother did not live nearby but when we did see her, she was all you would expect a grandmother to be. When I was 10 years old, my grandmother who was young and in good health, suddenly passed away from a blood clot after a simple medical procedure. My grandmother had a hereditary disorder that caused her blood to clot easily, of which the doctors were unaware. A simple procedure that was not statistically risky turned out fatal for my dear grandmother. At this young age I was faced with the reality that we are not guaranteed tomorrow. This event started a pattern of fear in my life.

It is easier for fear to take root after a traumatic experience. After that loss, I remember struggling with the fear of my parents dying. I clearly remember one night in particular. My parents had gone out, and my younger sister and I were home with a babysitter. It was raining outside. I went up to my room and cried for a long time because I was so afraid that my parents would get in a car accident and die. None of that actually happened, but the fear of that worst-case scenario was intense enough that I still remember it today. Another time in high school, a friend had to drive through a snowstorm after dropping me off, and I remember being on the edge of my seat until he called to tell me he made it home safely. You likely have experienced similar fears as the result of weather conditions that pose a serious threat to drivers or other situations that appear to pose a threat of physical harm. In both of these cases, my fear subsided as soon as I was assured that my loved ones were safe.

However, sometimes fears can be irrational. When fear doesn't match the situation's perceived risk, or when fear lasts beyond the assurance of safety, anxiety can set in. For instance, shortly after I got married, I began to feel dependent on my husband, and the fear of him dying gripped me. I stayed awake at night, crying and praying that God would not take him from me. The simple childhood fear that my parents might be hurt by driving through a rainstorm and actually experiencing the death of a friend from my youth group combined into full blown paralyzing anxiety. However, in this case, my anxiety was not necessarily the result of a disorder, rather it may have been spiritually driven as a result of my fear; it was very likely a spiritual attack.

This fear escalated and spread into an all-consuming fear that something would happen to someone in my family. That's when I started to see that there was something spiritual at work in my life. During what should have been a fun season as a newlywed, I was experiencing very little joy. I was so afraid of what could happen that it was hard to enjoy living in the moment. I sought prayer from others and spent time with the Lord trying to discern what was stealing my joy and paralyzing my mind in fear.

Through prayer, God allowed my heart to ask some of the deepest questions. Since I had experienced the loss of my friend, Josh, in a car accident, I was confronted with the possibility that my husband could die in some kind of fatal accident. Statistically, my husband was not going to die in a fatal accident; however, that simple data-driven fact did not ease my anxiety. I confronted my fear and anxieties by asking myself, *What if something does happen to my husband? Would I still love the Lord? Would I still trust Him? Did I believe the Holy Spirit would comfort me? Did I believe that God would provide for me? Would Jesus redeem the various tragedies I had running through my mind if they did indeed happen? Could I survive on my relationship with God alone if I lost everything? Was I willing to endure even the worst things for the glory of God?* I spent many heart wrenching prayer sessions in the middle of the night to find my heart's answers to these questions. I had to wrestle with my desire to be in control and avoid hardship, but when I was finally able to bring my will into agreement with my heart, I had an asnwer to all of these questions.

One by one I agreed to believe the promises of God, and as I did, the fear and anxiety lifted. Holding onto this perspective allowed me to smolder the fear of a loved one dying and the anxiety of difficult things happening. I could start enjoying my life again. Had I not challenged my fear and anxiety, I likely would still be suffering under the weight of them. Friend, this experience was certainly spiritual in nature. I did not seek counseling at that point

PERSPECTIVE

in my life, and I was not yet taking any medication. Fighting off Satan, wrestling my sinful nature, and submitting my human condition to Christ brought me relief. However, if you are experiencing the level of pain and fear that I was at that time, there is no shame in seeking professional or medical help.

New Circumstances Bring Up Old Fears

As God started teaching me about fear, I started to develop the perspective that God was all I needed and God's glory was my ultimate foundation. I gained strength from these truths. However, ten years and a few more traumatic experiences later, a new circumstance brought up an old fear. I was pregnant with my third baby, and this time my fear was not fear emerging from a wife's heart but rather fear emerging from the heart of a mama.

Both my first and second born children faced life threatening situations as infants. When my first son was ten days old he aspirated vomit which threatened his life. Luckily my son was sleeping in our bedroom when he aspirated so we heard his struggle immediately. We called 911, and we watched as he coughed, screamed and periodically stopped breathing while we waited for an ambulance. The paramedics arrived and took him directly to the hospital. As I waited to fully understand the risk to my son's life, I pleaded with God to allow my son to live. When I arrived at the ER, I saw my son's limp body on the hospital bed as medical professionals flopped him around during the intubation process. He was in the ICU for five days as we waited to know if he would ever be strong enough to breathe on his own again. I felt completely out of control as I prayed for God to save my son. I knew it was up to God because I couldn't do anything to protect him. After five days of enduring multiple tests, the doctors decided that he was okay and what happened to him was simply a fluke. He was discharged within 12 hours of being taken off of his breathing machine, and we were able to take our little blessing home.

That terrifying experience left a scar on my mama heart. I knew all too well that the life of an infant is incredibly fragile. When I was pregnant with my second born, I again had to face the gut-wrenching reality that an infant's life is incredibly precious. During my daughter's labor and delivery, she had the cord wrapped around her neck, and her left shoulder got stuck in my pelvic bone. The nurses had to push and pull on top of my belly to try to reposition her as I pushed through the contractions. Things were not progressing as they should, and so the emergency labor and delivery team arrived to coach me to continually push without any breaks between contractions. My body was so fatigued that I could no longer feel the pushing. The climate of the room was so chaotic and intense that I knew my daughter's life was at risk. I felt completely out of control, and I prayed "Help me! If she doesn't come out now she will die." I knew it was up to God because I couldn't do anything more to protect her. After a couple minutes she was wiggled free from my pelvic bone and delivered safely. Although she came out blue and quiet, after a short time of oxygen support she started crying, and I was able to hold my precious gift from God.

Skipping forward about 4 years to my third pregnancy, I realized that those previous traumatic memories brought with them many fears and emotions. I thought I had thoroughly tackled my anxiety, but during my third pregnancy, new layers of intense fear began to emerge. I thought I had a solid perspective on God's sovereignty. I thought I had surrendered my fear through those past trials. But my third pregnancy brought with it a new set of circumstances that challenged my ability to surrender my fear. As the doctors reviewed my chart they noted my family history of a blood disorder, and they noted the events of my previous pregnancy with my daughter. These circumstances caused me to face a new set of risks and ultimately a new set of choices. I had to choose between a cesarean delivery that could put my life at risk because of the possible blood disorder or a natural birth that could put my baby's life at risk due to the complications I experienced delivering my daughter. Weighing my choices, I entered a new place of fear.

I decided to risk my life instead of the baby's and proceed with the cesarean delivery. In that time I held on with desperation to what I had learned about God's sovereignty. During the day, I was able to mostly stifle the fear that the delivery might leave my kids motherless. I knew that if it was God's plan for me not to survive the C-section, then He would take care of everyone in my life. By that point in our lives, we had a living will, life insurance plans, and our parents lived next door. Because of God's provisions, I knew that my immediate family would be taken care of if something happened to me. That brought me some aspect of peace. I also found comfort in knowing that I had accomplished what I dreamt of accomplishing in my life. I wanted to be married, have children and start a Christian counseling center. My dreams were a reality. With my family surrounded in support and my business operating efficiently, the threats posed by my third pregnancy made me think that maybe I indeed was living my last earthly days.

Despite the fact that the risk of losing my life was small, and though I kept my eyes on the Lord during the day and in my quiet, sleepless nights, I still felt afraid. I spent time writing letters to my children, just in case I didn't survive the operation, and I also asked a good friend to intentionally spend time with my daughter who would be left as the only girl in a family of boys. Though I had peace that God would redeem my family's potential pain, I was also sad. I knew then and I know now that my family needs God more than they need me, and God redeems all of the pain or loss that we experience. However, my heart was still heavy. I was not afraid to die. I felt afraid for the pain that my children may have to endure. The weight of their possible sadness felt like too much to bear alone in the middle of the night, so I prayed often.

I wrestled with this throughout my pregnancy. Through that time, God gave me strength and peace so that I could still function. Ultimately my water broke, and the decision had been made for me to have a C-section. That is when the fear really heightened. I had a flood of thoughts that my children might not see me again, that I would miss seeing them grow up, and that I would not get to see the amazing plans that God has for their lives, and I feared that I may never get to meet the precious little man I had been growing for nine months. As soon as my water broke, the adrenaline started, and my husband held me while I cried. I found the strength to cast my eyes to the Lord, and I went into my kids' rooms as they slept. I prayed a prayer of blessing and protection over them, and I desperately prayed that I would get to watch them grow.

When we got to the hospital, the nurses provided me with information that surprised me. This new information showed that the risk to the baby was much lower than my OB originally thought. The hospital staff suggested that we do not move forward with the C-section. They gave us all of the information and all of our options, and it was up to us to decide. While the stakes were high and the clock was ticking as I labored, my husband and I took the time to pray about our decision. God answered our prayers just in time. With our emotions running high, God steadied my heart and provided guidance by the Holy Spirit, ultimately leading us against the C-section. In the end, everything was fine. Our baby was born healthy, and neither of us endured any complications.

During those pregnancy months, I still believed that God would take care of my family if something were to happen to me. I still believed God's glory would supersede the outcome, but that did not mean that I was completely absent of the emotion of fear. Some emotions of fear are normal. Some fear is part of survival. If we never feel fear, we would never know when it was time to run away from a threat of danger. Fear can be a healthy reaction to a reasonable level of risk or threat. But when fear bleeds into anxiety and impacts thought patterns and one's ability to function, we must seek the Holy Spirit in order to die to the flesh that is irrationally controlling us. Rather than living out of a fear of pain, we must pray and ask God for direction knowing that His ways are better than our ways.

Since the children have flesh and blood, he too shared in their humanity so that by his death he might break the power of him who holds the power of death—that is, the devil— and free those who all their lives were held in slavery by their fear of death. For surely it is not angels he helps, but Abraham's descendants.

(Hebrews 2:14–16)

The fear of death can keep us in bondage and keep us from living out God's calling in our lives with peace and confidence. If you have a fear of dying, think of this: If the worst happened and you died (which you will someday), and if you have accepted Jesus' free gift of salvation, you will be in a better place. Your death will leave those you love in pain, but you will have no more tears. Those who are left here can be comforted by the Holy Spirit. He can pull them closer to Himself, and He can teach them an intimacy with Him that they never experienced before. He can redeem their pain for His glory and their good.

Friend, if fear consumes your mind, if it impacts your ability to function, or if it makes you question God's sovereignty in your life, you may need to examine your perspective. If you make decisions out of fear, or if you act out of fear against the direction of the Holy Spirit, then you need to consider whether or not you are using the Bible to filter your thoughts. Consider asking yourself these questions:

- Have I fully surrendered my life to Christ?
- Am I willing to trust God with my life and my future?
- Do I love Jesus so much that I am willing to endure possible pain or hardship?
- Do I trust Jesus that He will take care of me?
- Do I trust that no matter what happens, Jesus will redeem my pain for His glory?
- Is God's glory my top priority?

Living Without Fear

Though most of us are impressed by stories of martyrdom, we may simultaneously feel grateful and blessed that we don't live in

133

a situation in which we have to worry about being put to death because of our faith. Some of us even wonder if our faith is strong enough to withstand a physical death threat if we were ever in the position to stand for Christ at the risk of our lives. The Holy Spirit can free you from all your fears.

In Luke Chapter 22, the disciple Peter struggled to have this perspective during his Christian life. Three times he denied Jesus even after Jesus warned Peter that he would. Nonetheless, Jesus did not reject Peter, and Peter took the opportunity to repent. Jesus asked Peter three times if he loved Him to which Peter replied that he did every time. When you are faced with a threat, ask yourself, "Do I believe Jesus' teachings?" and "Am I committed to follow Jesus regardless of what happens to me or my loved ones?" If you can answer yes to those questions, your fear will begin to subside. Take the chance in your life to spend time with Jesus and tell Him, "Yes, I love you and will follow you no matter what might come my way." This yes was life-changing for me in letting go of the fear in my life.

As we read in Acts, Peter then went on to be a bold ambassador for Christ, focused on God's eternal plan. He traveled to spread the gospel, preaching to thousands, and he eventually was killed for his faith. We see Peter, the same man who was once so filled with fear for his safety that he denied Christ three times, become so sure of God's eternal plan for his life that being imprisoned for the gospel didn't appear to cause him fear or anxiety.

In Acts 12, Peter is imprisoned for preaching the gospel. While in prison, Peter is found sleeping like a baby.

Suddenly an angel of the Lord appeared and a light shone in the cell. He struck Peter on the side and woke him up.

"Quick, get up!" he said, and the chains fell off Peter's wrists.

(Acts 12:7)

Peter was sleeping so soundly that the angel had to strike him to wake him. His counterpart James had just been beheaded for the same crime, so one would think that Peter would be filled with fear and anxiety as he waited. Yet Peter managed to sleep soundly. This is astonishing to me as one who knows sleepless nights well.

The change we see in Peter is amazing. According to some Bible Commentaries, some Scholars beleive that that Peter no longer feared for his life despite the inevitable threat of being beheaded for spreading the good news of Jesus. Peter had fully surrendered his life to Christ, and he trusted God's plan regardless of the harm that he might experience as a result of that trust. If Peter had been afraid, he would likely not have been able to sleep so soundly. Would you have slept soundly?

Are you able to face your fears with a willingness to do whatever it takes or endure whatever pain might come all for the glory of God? In some ways, if we allow ourselves to become too fearful or worrisome about what difficult things might happen, because of our fear, we attempt to maintain control of it in our own minds rather than surrendering that part of our lives to Christ.

I believe it is possible to resist fear even when medical tests or the circumstances of life stresses point to the worst possible outcomes. Because I am a follower of Christ, I know ultimately that every day that I am breathing is a gift, and God's glory is my top priority. I know He will comfort and take care of my family. In our most painful experiences God can bring about the most beautiful redemption and draws us closer to Him.

The Holy Spirit helps me repent of fear. After much time spent wrestling my selfish sinful nature, a nature that wants to control things and know the outcomes, a nature that would rather not take risks, I have been able to come to a place of surrendering my fear to the Lord.

- With all of my readers as witnesses I confess to Jesus:
- Yes I love you enough to endure pain
- Yes I love you enough to endure rejection
- Yes I love you enough to give up everything
- Yes I love you enough to endure death of myself or a loved one
- Yes I love you enough to abandon my plans to follow yours
- Yes I love you Lord, Here I am, send me

These confessions of faith point to the work of the Holy Spirit breaking the chains of fear in my life.

I share this to encourage you that it is possible to embrace a perspective of faith that snuffs out out the fear in your life. No matter what pain, loss, stress, persecution, injury, or death will happen in your life, God's glory and God's bigger plan is worth whatever pain you or your loved ones might endure.

Breaking the Stronghold of Fear

Fear is a common stronghold that Satan uses to keep us distracted from the mission that God has given us. When we are afraid of something, we put a lot of effort into avoiding it. We believe lies and develop ways of thinking that subconsciously are supposed to protect us from whatever we fear, but ultimately they keep us prisoner. If we are afraid of not having enough money, we work countless hours and take whatever means necessary to move up the ladder. If we are afraid of getting sick, we may wash our hands constantly, take many expensive supplements, or obsess over weight and blood tests. If we are afraid of something bad happening to our kids, we shelter them beyond what's developmentally appropriate. If we are afraid of being rejected because of our appearance, we will spend endless money and time to enhance our appearance. If we are afraid of being rejected for who we are, we work to always follow proper etiquette and never let people see the real us.

> The Lord is my light and my salvation—whom shall I fear?
> The Lord is the stronghold of my life—of whom shall I be afraid?
>
> (Psalm 27:1)

When fear is your stronghold, a misaligned perspective develops. This perspective causes you to think that you have control over something even when you don't. We think we are in control of how much money we make, when the reality is that a turn in the economy, a layoff, or bankruptcy could be right around the corner. We think we are in control of how we look, when the reality is that beauty standards are manufactured, and we are immersed in a beauty culture that profits from fueling negative self-image. We think we can control what our kids experience and the outcomes of each situation, and we forget that God's plan for our kids' lives is actually better than our plans for them. We forget that the all-powerful God who created the universe, set everything in motion, and established a plan to save us from the sin that we brought onto ourselves, is the same all-powerful God who has a purpose and a plan for each of us. We lose touch with the magnitude of Christ's sacrifice—He died and rose from the dead, brought people from death to life, and sent us Divine support and favor. It is that majestic Jesus who is in control of our problems too.

> Look at the birds of the air; they do not sow or reap or store away in barns, and yet your heavenly Father feeds them. Are you not much more valuable than they? Can any one of you by worrying add a single hour to your life?
> (Matthew 6:26–27)

Friend, I want to encourage you to think about those verses. It's easy to read them and not think too much about them. But when we really consider what they are saying to us, we can ask ourselves the questions: What do we have to be afraid of, and what do we have to worry about? If we truly grasp the perspective of having complete trust in the Almighty Creator of the universe, and if we truly surrender to that trust, then what is there to be afraid of?

We are so afraid to give up control, and yet we know that we cannot plan our lives better than God can. We hold onto that control, and it paralyzes us. By grasping for what only God can control, we hinder our joy and our ability to grow in Christ. Friend, let go of control. Let go of fear. I urge you to embrace a perspective that God knows better than you do, and even if something difficult comes your way, it is worth the temporary pain and suffering, because God can work out His glory through you.

CHAPTER 9

PERSPECTIVE TO FACE TRIALS AND ANXIETY

When we face trials or anxieties, it is important to understand that God has a plan for us. Difficult things are happening all around us, sometimes because of the sin in this world and sometimes because of natural consequences. Many times it is a mix of both. When trials and anxieties arise, we have an opportunity to gain deeper intimacy with God by leaning into Him and searching for a lesson we can learn rather than pushing Him away and stewing in negative feelings.

What are Trials?

The Bible tells us that trials are to be met with joy (James 1:2). Trials are things that happen in our lives that we have to endure, often due to the sin of others or the consequences of living in a fallen world. They often lead us to a place or a situation in which we need to fully depend on God. Without trials, we would not get to the same deep understanding of our need for God. Often times in trials our flesh wants to push God away. Anger and a skewed perspective often consume us when struggles persist. However, trials invite us to lean into the Holy Spirit for strength. Doing so allows us to search for purpose and God's bigger plan.

Many of us think that God should protect us from our trials and pain, but the Bible doesn't tell us that we will not have trials and suffering in this life (1 Peter 4:12, 1 Peter 5:6–11). Our flesh will want to hide from trials and will want to try to take control of the situation in hopes of avoiding pain. However, we must draw close to the Lord and allow Him to strengthen our hearts through the trials we endure.

In hard times, even though we fight our flesh and we try to draw near to the Lord, sometimes it can seem as if He has pulled away from us. Friend, please know that God is not absent in those quiet times when you do not feel Him close to you. He does some of His most profound work when we cannot see what He is doing. When you think He is not doing anything, He is behind the scenes working out details that you wouldn't even have thought to consider. God is faithful and trustworthy, and He is always with you. It is important to keep pressing in, and in time, you will see His work and feel His comfort.

My Trials

> Dear friends, do not be surprised at the fiery ordeal that has come on you to test you, as though something strange were happening to you. But rejoice inasmuch as you participate in the sufferings of Christ, so that you may be overjoyed when his glory is revealed.
>
> (1 Peter 4:12–13)

Early in our marriage when Mike struggled with anxiety and

depression, I was going through a trial. He was going through his own pain and suffering, struggling with his own thoughts and fears, but for me, I was dealing with the trial of watching him suffer. I felt like he should be able to do something to get himself out of the anxiety and depression that was leaving him with an inability to function. This caused me great pain. Often anxiety and trials go together, but sometimes they exist independent of the other. The Holy Spirit certainly strengthened me during that time of trial. I learned how to trust in God for our future. I learned how to trust God's leading in my life even when things do not seem to make sense. I learned the importance of patience, as I experienced my patience growing a little at a time. But I initially endured that trial with more anger and anxiety than trust and strength.

A few years later I faced another trial that grew my patience and my trust in God's plan. When our first born was 8 months old, he started wheezing whenever he suffered a cold virus. Having watched him almost choke to death when he was only 10 days old, this new experience of wheezing proved especially challenging to endure. We ended up in the doctor's office, urgent care, and the emergency room more times than I can remember. Any little virus would cause his lungs and breathing to struggle. We would be up all night monitoring his breathing, giving him breathing treatments, and sitting in steam showers.

As a first time mama, this was terrifying. It is scary watching and listening to your child struggle to breathe. Now that I have three children and much more experience discerning when one of my kids needs medical attention, I am more confident and less worried when the cold virus visits our house. But those early parenting years rattled me.

Through the years I have asked myself the question, "Do I trust God regardless of the future?" Having already worked through this question in the past, I found it easier to have patience and trust while I was dealing with those early months and years of watching my son suffer. Since I already had confidence in God's plans, this trial, though difficult, was not anxiety-provoking for me. I had peace that although we had to continually give my son treatments, he was never actually in danger. I also learned how to walk through a difficult situation while relying on God's strength to get me through.

When I think back to that time, I know I got through it because of the strength of the Holy Spirit. I prayed every night that my son would grow up healthy and strong; I still do. I also knew that the time I had with my son was precious and not guaranteed. I was able to focus on the joy of being his mama amidst the trial, even enduring countless trips to urgent care. God gave me strength to endure that difficult season, and by His grace, my son has outgrown the issue.

Purpose in Trials

God always brings about purpose in our trials. There are many examples in the Bible of people going through trials. One of the most profound examples is that of Job from the book of Job. Job had everything that was dear to him taken away. His house, his riches, his livelihood, and even his sons—Job lost it all. During this tragic season of loss, Job's friends and his wife were not supportive. They wanted Job to turn away from God, but instead Job praised God. Job had a proper perspective that everything that he had was from the Lord, and if the Lord allowed it to be taken away, who was he to complain about it?

- Do you have Job's perspective when you lose something that is dear to you or when you go through a trial?
- What about something that simply makes your life more convenient—what is your perspective when something like that is taken away from you?
- Are you able to see all the blessings in your life as given to you by the Lord, or do you feel like you have earned them and deserve them?
- Are you able to face your trials in a way that allows you to also keep your joy in the moment?

In all this you greatly rejoice, though now for a little while you may have had to suffer grief in all kinds of trials. These have come so that the proven genuineness of your faith— of greater worth than gold, which perishes even though refined by fire—may result in praise, glory and honor when Jesus Christ is revealed.

(1 Peter 1:6–7)

Through the years of counseling clients and supervising therapists, I have been privy to countless tragedies in people's lives. The hurt and pain that I have witnessed is overwhelming. This is part of the job. It takes a certain type of person with a clear calling on their life to be in this profession without wavering. Over the years, questions of God have come up as I sat with people in their pain. Why does God allow this to happen? Why would God not stop people from hurting each other? The answers to these questions go back to having an eternal perspective and understanding that trials grow our faith.

To comprehend the answers to these questions, you must understand that the God who knows all—who knows the needs of everyone and desires to save the lost—is sovereign over everything that happens. Many times things happen, even difficult things happen, because the situation or circumstance will ultimately bring glory to God. Many times, things happen that make our lives more painful or more difficult.

God does not promise us an easy life. Some of our clients have lost loved ones, been sexually or physically assaulted, witnessed wars, or endured so many other terrible things. When those people are willing to experience deeper intimacy with God and put their trust in Him even after a tragedy, they become powerful and profound witnesses to who God is. When people are open and honest with others about their tragic and painful experiences, opportunity arises for the hearts of others to soften and turn to the Lord. As often as I have heard the question, "Why would God let this happen," I have also heard the sentiment, "God allowed it to happen to me so I can help others through it." Though this conclusion is usually drawn after a person has worked through their pain, it is a testament to the truth that there is purpose to the pain.

As a therapist, I have witnessed many clients draw this conclusion during their own time spent with the Lord. The healing process moves a suffering person to a deeper level of healing when that person understands that God allowed their pain in order to bring glory to Himself. The redemption of that pain can be transformative both for the one who endured the pain and for those who witness the process toward redemption. Many times God uses pain to call the unsaved to Himself. Having a biblical perspective about the difficult things that happen in this world helps me to serve all of my clients regardless of their faith, and it allows me to hear and witness so much pain and horror without experiencing anxiety myself.

What is Anxiety?

It is natural when we see difficult things happen to other people to notice that those things could happen to us as well. Movies, television shows, and especially the news all present to us the fallen scenarios of this sinful world, and they remind us that difficult things do happen to people. This is a fairly obvious observation. However, this can turn problematic when we let that observation evolve into more intense thoughts about how bad it would be if those things happened to us. It is a problem when the question, "How would I survive if x, y, or z happened to me" results in us worrying excessively about the possibility of enduring such pain.

Anxiety is different from a trial because anxiety is not something that we must endure in order to grow. Anxiety is something that stunts growth. Anxiety is the feeling of tension and unrest that occurs with the anticipation of something bad happening. Anxiety leads to the experience of fear and dread. When we are anxious we anticipate something difficult without much evidence that it will happen. It is an emotional response to the thoughts of anticipation. Typically there is also a physical response to anxious emotions, such as shortness of breath, tight muscles, rapid heart rate, increased adrenaline, brain fog, or anger.

This anticipation creates an irrational feeling of fear and is often overwhelming. The secular world has mostly seen anxiety as an imbalance in brain chemicals that we have no control over.

More recently therapeutic models have shown that changing the things that we think and making an effort to be mindful of the present moment can change our brain. Focusing on the present and not the past or the future is a biblical concept. Psychology has adapted this concept and has developed a treatment model called mindfulness. Therefore the secular world is starting to agree that we can be in control of these thoughts and ultimately our brain functioning.

From a Christian perspective, anxiety is something that is brought up by our own sinfulness because the Bible tells us not to worry. We are told not to fear and not to be anxious because God is in control and we must trust Him to take care of our situations (Matthew 6:25, Luke 12:22–31, Psalm 46:10, Psalm 26:3, Philippians 4:19). Simply put, because we live in a sinful world, trials exist and difficult things do happen, but we are to put our trust in God so that we will not be anxious and afraid. We are to endure trials with grace and grow in faith accordingly and not allow them to stir up anxious thoughts within us. I do understand that this is much easier said than done.

Anxious Thoughts and Your Brain

One scientific factor in anxiety and depression is the neural pathways that have been created in your brain. Neural pathways are the part of your nervous system that send information from one part of your body to another. When it comes to mental health, information is transferred back and forth from the amygdala to the hippocampus, and these two parts of the brain play the largest role in emotional processing. As you continue to have the same thoughts over and over, your brain establishes pathways from these two parts that make it easy to continue on that same thought path next time. So the more you have the same thoughts, the easier it is to continue them and the harder it is to divert them.

Neural pathways in your brain are like a walking path through the woods. Once you have walked on it a few times and the shrubs are out of the way, that path becomes the easiest path to take. So when something happens that increases your emotions and adrenaline, it is as if you have brought your bike to the woods. In trying to ride your bike, it is nearly impossible to take a different path through the woods because now you are traveling more quickly. Your bike likely can't fit through an overgrown pathway, therefore you will take the already established path as you bicycle through the woods.

Consider a situation in which something does not go your way. It is easy to start thinking, "See, nothing ever goes right for me," "I am just a failure," and "Life is never going to get easier" when you have already thought these things many times before. In fact, your brain will automatically continue down the same path until you intentionally redirect your thoughts. The more emotion, stress, and adrenaline you have in a situation, the faster and farther your brain will go down these negative trains of thought.

So, just like in the woods, in order to create a new path for your thoughts, you cannot be on your bike of emotion, so-to-speak. If you can be calm and intentional, you can slowly and carefully take a more positive path that has not yet been established. You can take the time to avoid any hazardous shrubs, ensure your direction is on point, and lay down a new healthier pathway. You can replace your negative and anxious thought patterns with thoughts such as, "Things didn't go my way, but I can adjust," "This might be another struggle, but I can learn from it," and "God must have a purpose in this." I believe this is partly why the Bible tells us to take every thought captive and make it submissive to Christ (2 Corinthians 10:5). We have to slowly plan out strategic pathways that are aligned with Christ, or we will find ourselves overwhelmed and lost in the middle of the woods, turned in the wrong direction.

Research has also found that when our memories and thoughts are accompanied by fear and anxiety, we remember them more clearly than memories and thoughts that are accompanied by other feelings. When we have fear or anxiety, our stress hormone is excreted in our brains which makes us more alert. This is all a part of the fight or flight response, which God created in us to stay safe in the face of actual danger. Our brain is motivated to remember fearful events and thoughts as a mechanism for daily survival.

When we are not taking our thoughts captive, we tend to have an abundance of negative thoughts. We over-interpret our situations as terrible, stressful, or overwhelming because we are trying to take control of the situation instead of giving it to God. This causes negative neural pathways to be reinforced, and it can cause mental illness in our brain chemistry.

The more and more we think negative and anxious thoughts, the easier those thoughts become accessible to us. In other words, the more we think fearfully, the more we will experience fear. Without intentional intervention for negative thoughts (like taking our thoughts captive and submitting them to God's truth), the worse our anxieties will become. Without intervention, our fears will start to appear to be facts and our negative thoughts will be reinforced by our brain chemicals.

My Anxieties

I have struggled with different anxieties over the years. I have shared a bit about my anxieties regarding parenting and my fear of difficult things happening but one of my biggest triggers for anxiety is about money and finances. When God called us to start our own business, we had to rely heavily on our savings to stay financially afloat. Additionally, we were initially paying for business related expenses out of our own pocket. It took longer than I expected for us to break even let alone for us to make any profit at all. For a number of years I worked without any paycheck, and we watched nervously as the money we owed on our business loan grew and grew.

This was a terrifying experience for me as one who worried about money often. I told my counselor that it actually felt traumatic because when financial struggles arise, I can actually feel the stress hormones, adrenaline and cortisol, flowing through my veins. My worry about spending and saving money is an everyday struggle.

Through the process of building a low-margin, high expense, third-party payer business from the ground up, I have learned that money is not our safety net. God is our safety net and he has provided for my family in many unconventional ways. For instance, rather than buying an expensive engagement ring, I received my grandmother's diamond, minimizing the cost of that otherwise large expense. A pastor sold a car to us below trade-in value. An investor wrote off our business debt stating that God led him to help us.

Even after all of these unconventional provisions, it is still easy for me to worry about money when I am focused on it. I have to focus on God. I have to remember that, although we are business owners and are always at risk of skipping a paycheck, God will provide for what we need now and in the future. He has always provided for us.

> Cast all your anxiety on him because he cares for you.
>
> (1 Peter 5:7)

> And my God will meet all your needs according to the riches of his glory in Christ Jesus.
>
> (Philippians 4:19)

God wants us to be good stewards of what we have, invest our money instead of squandering it away, and be generous with our money (1 Timothy 6:17, Proverbs 10:4–5, Proverbs 13:11, 1 Corinthians 16:2). Many times He provides for our future with the money that we saved. Other times He provides for our future in unforeseen ways. God brought me to an understanding that if we lost everything because our business crashed, and if we lost our savings because of an unexpected expense, He will still provide. As long as I do my part in trying to be wise and intentional in how we spend the money God does bless us with, God will take care of the rest.

Starting our own business has resulted in many trials which turned into anxiousness because I wanted control of them. Much of this anxiety involved money and finances. Time and time again, I have to lay down my anxiety and trust God. It's no wonder the Bible tells us that it is impossible to serve both God and money. Money seems like it is our safety net, but the truth is that there is no security in money. God is our safety net. God is our security.

- Do you get anxious about money like I do sometimes?
- Do you serve God? Or do you serve money?

One technique used in therapy to help people with their anxiety is to ask, "What is the worst that could happen?" It is the therapist's job to help the client process the worst-case scenario. Part of that process is helping a client to not only accept the potential reality of the worst-case scenario, but it also helps the client to see a reality in which he/she would still be okay. This technique works because often people with anxiety have inflated the situation in their own mind since they are anticipating a future threat. When they realize that the worst-case scenario really isn't as bad as they've made it out to be, their anxiety begins to diminish. This technique is what I use with myself when I start to worry about money.

- So what do you worry about?
- Do you worry about injury, money, sickness, or rejection?
- What if you lose your job? Will God provide you with a new one? Will God prompt others to help you?
- What if someone gets sick and you have large medical bills? Will a hospital let you pay it over time or reduce your bill based on a sliding scale?
- What if you have a lawyer bill you have to pay? Would your family be able to help you out?
- What if you are rejected? Will God bring other people into your life? Will God reject you?

We can ask ourselves these questions in order to take the power away from our anxious minds.

Time and time again, I have seen God provide in unusual and miraculous ways. Society tells us that we must have a large savings account balance and a high-paying job with great benefits in order to be secure, but those things can easily be taken away. Our health, our stuff, our success, our apparent stability, our friends, and our family can all wither away. What cannot be taken away is God and His plans for our lives. We have to come to an understanding that God is in control, and He has a plan to care for both us and the ones we love, even in a worst-case scenario.

Be Anxious For Nothing

The Bible says:

> Do not be anxious about anything, but in every situation, by prayer and petition, with thanksgiving, present your requests to God.
>
> (Philippians 4:6)

This verse has been one that I hold onto when I am feeling stressed or anxious. Since I am an over thinker, I often have to analyze every little detail of something in order to feel good about it. When my brain circles around all the details and I become consumed with thoughts about how something might fail me or I might fail in something, I have to remind myself not to worry.

I have been very blessed with great in-laws. Both sides of our family are very supportive. My kids have an amazing support system for which we are so thankful. During my third pregnancy, I tried my best to prevent myself from feeling anxious about my fear surrounding the different medical complications the baby and I were facing. I talked with my mother-in-law about it, and in an effort to comfort me she told me, "Oh Charity, you can't think that way." At the time I knew she was right, but I still struggled. It seemed like an actual possibility that something bad could happen to the baby or me, and I couldn't really make an emotional connection to God's words, "Do not be anxious about anything." I pushed the anxiety away as best I could, and with God as my strength, I faced my fear. Nonetheless, I still remember feeling the tension and physical anxiety symptoms in my body during more than a few sleepless nights.

My mother-in-law's comfort was helpful in that I knew she was praying for me, and also I knew that she understood something that I did not understand. However, at the time, I couldn't figure out what I didn't understand. It wasn't until a year later, after everything went well with my pregnancy and my son's birth, that I got to see and understand how my mother-in-law's guidance to shut down the all-consuming negative thoughts can really make a difference in the moment, even when facing something scary.

A year after my anxiety-provoking pregnancy, labor, and delivery, my father-in-law discovered a suspicious spot on his skin that required a biopsy. Though the doctor seemed neutral about the potential results, my husband and I were still concerned. We were both worried, and admittedly, I was a tad anxious. But when I asked my mother-in-law about how she was doing, she said, "Well, worrying about it isn't going to change anything except to make me worried while we wait for the test results." She said, "There is nothing we can do until we know, so we will wait until we find out what we might have to do." She shared her perspective with such confidence. I could see that she was not merely pushing away the fear like I did when I faced my scary situation. Her steadiness was palpable, and it radiated onto me. As a therapist I realized that her solid faith in God created a perspective in her that is actually now taught in secular psychology as mindfulness. Of course psychology takes out the variable of God, but it is attempting to get the same peace by focusing on the present moment and not the past or the future.

Although I had heard the Scripture "Do not be anxious about anything" a hundred times before, in that moment, I could actually see how those words look when someone actually lives them. My mother-in-law was right. If she spent time thinking about and worrying about the outcome, it would only make those two weeks harder to endure. If my husband was the one waiting for biopsy results, I might have worked myself up thinking about the what ifs—what if he had to endure surgery, what if treatment didn't work, what if we lost him? But not my mother-in-law. She chose to not allow herself to entertain those thoughts, and as a result, she experienced peace in the waiting. Once the test results finally came back, we learned that the spot on his skin was not cancerous. Though the results could have been dramatically different, the worrying in the waiting would have only worsened either outcome.

Being anxious that difficult things might happen really is a waste of time. Difficult things will happen to us. The Bible tells us that. But the Bible also states:

> And we know that in all things God works for the good
> of those who love him, who have been called according to
> his purpose.
>
> (Romans 8:28)

Being anxious about nothing doesn't mean you pretend nothing difficult can happen, rather it means believing that when trials and hardships do happen, God will sustain you, get you through it, and deliver a purpose in it.

You might be like I was when my mother-in-law first encouraged me not to worry. You might intellectually believe this truth, but your heart and your emotions aren't catching up. I want to encourage you to pray and ask God to show you how not being anxious about anything can look in your life. According to the Bible, the things we suffer will work together with the rest of God's plan to bring glory to Him. God will give you a strength and a peace that surpasses all understanding if you can keep your thoughts and hopes locked on Him.

> When anxiety was great within me, your consolation brought me joy.
>
> (Psalm 94:19)

God asks us to surrender our whole lives to follow Him. We are to surrender our hopes, dreams, fears, and failures. We are to resist the temptation to control our lives.

- Are you willing to surrender your plan for God's higher plan? What about in the worst-case scenario? What if the plan means you might suffer? What if the plan costs you your life or the life of a loved one?
- What if, through your suffering or death, God is able to bring many people to Christ? Do you believe that God will give you strength to endure suffering?
- What if He allows the people who will be grieving your loss to reach new depths in their relationship with Christ

as a result of their grief? You will be with Jesus, right?

- Do you believe that God will take care of those you may leave behind?
- Do you believe God will take care of you if you lose your spouse?

Remember God's promises, and surrender your anxieties to Him.

There are so many things we can be anxious about, but God tells us not to be anxious about anything. The difficult things that happen are not things God does *to* us, rather they are things that God allows to happen *for* us. The stress, hardship, or suffering in a believer's life are not meant to destroy us, they strengthen us when we let them. They are meant to bring glory to Jesus, and they allow us to show the world that the Holy Spirit has the power to transform lives and comfort souls.

Friend, I want to encourage you to not waste your time being anxious in anticipation of something that might someday pose a threat. Do not fear the threats that are in front of you today, because God is bigger than any threat. Do not worry about what trials will come your way in life. Keep your perspective on Jesus and God's eternal purposes so you can experience a peace that you have never known before.

When we truly embrace God during our fear, anxiety, hardships, trials, suffering, or turmoil, He will teach us things that we could have never imagined about His love, grace, and strength. Our lives will be enriched in a way that we never would have thought possible. I am not saying that we will never be tempted to worry. But when we focus on the fear, anxiety, hardships, trials, suffering, and turmoil, we can't expect to also experience emotional, spiritual, or mental vibrancy and health. There will still be times of struggle in life.

What Jesus went through in the garden of Gethsemane was emotional turmoil. But believing that He will get us through no matter what happens brings with it a peace that silences anxiety and fear. Keep your eyes on the Lord's purposes through your suffering, and embrace the peace He wants to give you. Spend time in prayer and meditate on Scripture daily, and you will be strengthened by the Holy Spirit. You will find strength to fight your trials and anxiety.

CHAPTER 10

NEGATIVE FEELINGS AND DEPRESSION

As a therapist, a lot of my time is spent helping people process their emotions and feelings. This is important to do in order to look for underlying traumas or wounds and also in looking for misaligned thought processes and perspectives. These cause dysfunctional beliefs or lies that we tell ourselves. However, our culture has put an unhealthy emphasis on feelings. Culture tells us how we feel is the most important thing in evaluating our decisions. We often listen to other people to determine how something should make us feel. Sometimes when we have negative feelings about something, it has less to do with the situation and more to do with something coming from within us. Our feelings are filtered through our perspective, and if our perspective is misaligned, then our feelings will be also.

On the other hand, your emotions can be valid, and there are times that they can be red flags alerting you to something troubling or concerning. It is important to acknowledge how something makes you feel or you will never be able to process it and change the way it affects your life. We also can have negative emotions when there is conflict in our relationships, we are being mistreated, or we sense someone's evil intentions. These feelings can serve as red flags. Situations such as grief, loss, or charitable sorrow bring up strong emotions that are godly emotions and part of the normal human experience. Sometimes, however, we get carried away with superficial or selfish emotions, giving too much weight to feelings. These feelings are often a result of our own sin. For instance, sin can lead to damaging emotions when we poorly react to things not going our way, we engage in things that keep us distant from God, or we exhibit an impatient attitude toward a situation.

Cognitive Behavioral Therapy (CBT) is a therapy technique that acknowledges that feelings can change when one changes his or her thinking and actions. It incorporates interventions to help one change their thinking which in turn changes one's feelings. However, many of the therapies that are popular today focus heavily on feelings which makes it easy to get lost in a world of emotion that is fickle and subjective. The Enemy exploits our feelings and wants us to focus on our feelings exclusively as truth. If we take those feelings to God, the Holy Spirit can help illuminate the lies we are believing that cause us to experience otherwise fickle or subjective feelings.

Feelings Fluctuate

Our feelings are context dependent. When you are having a good day, you likely feel content. Then something small or insignificant happens and suddenly you feel stressed, angry, overwhelmed, sad, frustrated, rejected, or unloved. Likely you are still having a good day, but that small annoyance has shifted your perspective so that now your whole day seems off. It could be that nothing inherently bad happened but rather someone said something to you that, though well intentioned, triggered hurt from your past. Maybe you witnessed something that reminded you that the world can offer great disappointment. Maybe you are in a fine mood but a sudden whisper in your ear tells you that you are failing or that you are not good enough. Our moods can shift minute by minute for a multitude of reasons, and many of us experience mood swings without a clear recognition of what is causing us such emotional highs and lows.

Many times my kids have taught me the reality of fluctuating feelings, although I often forget this lesson and need to be reminded of it over and over again. There is something about that maternal instinct that wants to meet a child's needs and keep them happy, but one thing that I have struggled to remember is that feelings fluctuate. Feelings do not always define the reality of the situation even though they feel real in the moment. Because I am a working mom, I often have to fight the nag of mom guilt that comes with being away from my kids.

After a two-and-a-half week holiday break in which I was with my kids, I scheduled clients every evening for multiple consecutive nights. One particular night I got behind with my client schedule causing me to arrive home an hour later than usual. My husband assured me that the kids were fine, and that seemed to be the case when I finally arrived home. However, when it was time to put them to bed, you would have thought I had been away for months. My kids suddenly offered tear filled accusations that they never see me and I work too much and no one ever plays with them. My mama heart was heavy.

My oldest explained that he didn't like going to school anymore because he never gets to see me. He cried, and I assured him that we would find time to spend together the next day. When I woke him up early the next day so we could have breakfast together before I dropped him off at school, he told me that instead of breakfast with me, he would rather make sure that he got to school early so that he had time to talk to his friends. Of course I made him spend time with me anyway.

My daughter was different. Her guilt trip continued through the morning. She explained that she did not want our nanny to come again, and she wanted to spend the whole day with me. I took her for a special breakfast treat after dropping off my son at school so that she and I could spend some special time together. When the nanny arrived, my daughter seemed fine; the guilt trip was over.

As much as the change in their emotions relieved me of my mom guilt, it also made me a bit frustrated that I fell for it again. I fell for the tired and heightened emotions that many of us experience (especially kids) at the end of a long day. My mom guilt had me thinking that maybe I was not a good mom because I work too much or I don't spend the time with them that they need (not to mention, being a therapist sometimes makes it hard to be a mom because I tend to over analyze the fickle feelings of my kids).

By mid morning, my kids were acting completely themselves, and their apparent desperation to spend time with me had dissipated. But the sting of their ramblings and fickle emotions still stuck with me. The stress was mounting, and I argued with Mike because I thought that maybe I wasn't balancing life well enough to meet the needs of my kids.

It is slightly comical to consider the ways in which a child's fickle emotions can impact our own, but this is all the more reason to have caution when we allow our emotions to determine our perception of reality.

Although feelings are powerful, how you feel about something does not define it or make it true. This took me a while to learn. Emotions can either work for you or they can work against you. Often times we experience an abundance of emotions, and that throws us off track. As we learn in CBT, emotions rarely strike out of nowhere, rather they are usually preceded by a thought. Even if we only notice the emotion without realizing the thought that preceded it, most often there is a correlation that is taking place between our thoughts and emotions. CBT invites us to analyze the truthfulness of our thoughts in order to logically remove lies, assumptions, miscommunications, or half-truths. CBT encourages us to focus on the true facts about a situation. What CBT doesn't teach us is that Satan is the father of lies, and he aims to destroy us.

When I take the time to analyze my own negative thoughts and feelings with a biblical perspective, very often I can tell that they stem from one of Satan's lies. He seems to know that when he pushes a certain button, I become deeply lost in my negative feelings. To fight this I have had to change my perspective on my feelings. Many of my feelings are rooted in lies. In essence, my feelings are lying to me. This happens when I experience feelings that are triggered by those quiet roars from Satan or when I experience feelings that have been filtered through a misaligned perspective.

Feelings about your Marriage

A great example of how our feelings can lie to us is found in marriage relationships. Many married people report that after 6–12 months of marriage, the *feeling* that they had about their spouse has dissolved. Usually married couples can hang in there for a little while, but once stress enters a marriage, that changes. Character and personality traits that once seemed attractive become annoying and irritating. That combined with a culture that tells us we can fall in and out of love results in a society that supports divorce as an acceptable and even suggested option. According to our culture, the fate of marriage is dependent on emotions. Most couples enter marriage expecting to easily maintain that feeling of love without it fading away.

One research study compared newlyweds to married couples who had been together for many years. This study looked specifically at couples who reported a loss of that *feeling* although they had been married for a while. The study looked at the brain activity of both the newlyweds and the longer-married couples. Both brain scans showed similar brain activity. Specifically the brain scans looked for endorphins that are released when couples are in a romantic and intimate relationship because endorphins are what cause us to have positive feelings.

The longer-married couples showed the same endorphin releases as the newlyweds; however, the longer-married couples had adapted to living with the increased endorphins and therefore did not feel the effects of the endorphin release. In other words, neurologically, the longer-married couples experienced the same endorphin release as the newlyweds; however, it had become their norm. Combined with the added stress that comes with marriage, kids, and in-laws, it's no wonder the longer-married couples reported that they no longer *feel* love.

This same effect happens in drug addicts who require more and more of the substance in order to experience the initial high that hooked them to the drug. This study motivates me to encourage married couples to stop expecting to always feel the emotions they felt when they first fell in love. If a married couple can work through their issues, change their perspectives, and spend time on romantic dates, then they can experience a kind of love that is not based on fickle emotions, but rather a sacrificial love that is based on a true commitment.

Define Yourself By God, NOT Feelings

Our culture also tells us that if it feels right, do it. As Christians we know that is not how we are supposed to live. We know that although drinking an abundance of alcohol feels good for some people, it is actually destructive. We know that feeling accepted and approved by man is meaningless. We know that even if we feel different than our bodies tell us we are, God knit us together in our mother's womb, just the way we are. We know that although there may be certain urges such as overindulgence in alcohol, acting on inappropriate sexual thoughts, and many other things that we strongly want to indulge, we are to abstain. We abstain in order to stay within the boundaries that God has told us will keep us the most holy and healthy.

When we are presented with an opportunity for sin, such as sexual impurity, illegal substances, gossiping, or making money unethically, we are to choose what is right over what feels right. What feels right in the moment is not always right, and often what simply feels right may have many negative consequences that can impact us, others, and the future. If we can understand that and work to abstain from sinful things, God will show us the blessings of staying within His set boundaries.

- What things in your life do you need to work to avoid?
- What feels right to you even though it goes against what you know to be right in your heart?
- Can you work to abstain from indulging those feelings?

Just as we are to avoid feeling the excitement of sinful things, we also are to avoid the feelings of negativity and sinful thoughts. Satan uses our emotions in his battle plan to devour us. Do not let his roaring lies and negative thoughts persuade your fickle feelings. We do not have to feel overwhelmed, depressed, anxious, angry, disappointed, sad, or worthless.

> Finally, brothers and sisters, whatever is true, whatever is noble, whatever is right, whatever is pure, whatever is lovely, whatever is admirable—if anything is excellent or praiseworthy—think about such things. Whatever you have learned or received or heard from me, or seen in me—put it into practice. And the God of peace will be with you.
>
> (Philippians 4:8–9)

As a therapist, of course I believe that there is a mental health component of depression and negative feelings, but I also believe there is a spiritual component. When one draws close to the Lord and embraces a biblical perspective, they will experience an improvement in their mental health struggle with depression.

What is Depression?
Depression comes with a low mood along with lack of motivation, lack of joy in normally pleasurable activities, poor sleep,

low energy, and a negative self-image. According to science, depression is caused by many factors such as weak mood regulation by the brain, genetic vulnerability, stress, or medical conditions. Research has shown that the hippocampus—which plays an important role in emotion regulation—is smaller in those that experience depression, and that stress is one of the main factors for the onset of depression.

The hormones that your body releases when you are stressed suppresses the production of new neurons in the hippocampus, and because of this, research connects stress with low mood. As we continue to repeat the same negative thoughts over and over we create neural pathways that will make it easier for our brain to arrive at the same destination—a low mood caused by negative thoughts and feelings. Some researchers believe that mood only improves as new, balanced, and positive thought patterns, or neural pathways, are formed.

Although medication is one treatment option to improve neuro communications, treatments such as CBT have shown that you can create new thought patterns. These new thought patterns create new neural pathways by intentionally focusing on what you are thinking, and analyzing the evidence that seems to support each negative thought. From a biblical perspective, we are to take every thought captive and make it submissive to Christ (2 Corinthians 10:5), and we are to think about things that are positive (Philippians 4:8). Practicing those two cognitive habits, according to research, forms new neural pathways and in turn improves mood and feelings of depression.

Some of my clients who are battling clinical depression and anxiety are unaware of the impact that the spiritual realm has on his or her mental health struggles. Gaining a strong understanding of who God is, how much He loves you, and the purpose for your existence can help you surrender your stress to God and think positively. I would claim that being able to have a biblical perspective will change the way you react to stressors. You will be able to experience a stressor, including the chemical reaction of the stress hormones released in your body, and still quickly return to normal when you release your burden to Christ.

The alternative to this is to experience a stressor, release the stress hormones, continue to feel stressed, continue to release stress hormones, analyze, overthink, and feel responsible. This alternative leads to experiencing the long term effect of the stress hormone which can interrupt a healthy functioning hippocampus. By creating new and positive neural pathways, you are supporting the healthy growth of your hippocampus, and this has been linked to an improved mood.

It is important to remember that, in addition to the above factors, there is another explanation to our issues with anxiety and depression. Sometimes we are experiencing a spiritual attack. No matter how much medication and clinical treatment one seeks, it won't provide full healing when the root of the issue is a spiritual one. As a Christian therapist, if I neglect the spiritual battle we are in and the spiritual side of depression, my client will miss out on treatment of the whole person. In order to best assist my clients in establishing new patterns of thought and new neural pathways, we must address the feelings and beliefs they have about themselves, others, and God. Ultimately this improves the chemicals in the brain that affect mood.

Sometimes we miss the blessing of working through our negative feelings with God because we have masked the spiritual component of our negative feelings. We do this by simply medicating or by believing that our negative feelings are just a brain chemical issue. For some people, medication and talk therapy does not lead to healing. As soon as the medication and therapy ceases, the anxiety and depression returns. There are times when medications are useful and helpful, but I believe that as a child of God, many things have a spiritual cause and need a spiritual cure.

In Luke 13 we read the story of Jesus healing a woman who had been crippled for 18 years. This story sheds light on the significance of the spiritual battle that is at war with our physical and mental health.

In the story, the crippled woman has been "bent over" for 18 years. Her spine was literally bent over. All she could do was look at the ground. She was never able to see the whole picture around her. Having been afflicted for so long, she likely sought many worldly solutions to try to straighten out her back. In the story she encounters Jesus, and He miraculously heals her. Her medical problem required a spiritual solution. While her problem was physical on the outside, it was spiritual on the inside.

The Bible tells us that she was bent over because she was "crippled by a spirit...." In order for her to lose the spirit and straighten up, she had to encounter Jesus. The Bible does not lead us to believe that she had done something wrong to cause her affliction. Nonetheless, her affliction was rooted in the spiritual realm, and an encounter with Christ the Messiah was the solution.

As I heard this story explained, it hit me. How often is our perspective, our mood, or our mental health skewed because the root cause is spiritual? If this woman could have been bent over physically for so long without relief, how likely is it that we might have a kink in our thinking or a perspective that needs to be straightened out in order for our mental or emotional health to be healed? Just like the crippled woman, we experience many emotional or spiritual things that force our heads to the ground, making it seem impossible to look up to God. While we look down at the ground we assume our problem is rooted in physical or mental health instead of realizing the spiritual cause. Although many times depression is caused my a biological issue, if we are like this woman, we may not have a medical problem but a spiritual one, and as such its prescription is an encounter with Jesus.

Overcoming Depression with your Perspective

I once heard a pastor explain that anxiety and depression are a result of selfish thinking. As a therapist I can understand if that statement is offensive, especially if you are struggling with anxiety or depression. Yet over the years I have started to understand what selfish thinking has to do with anxiety and depression.

Science shows that depression is a legitimate medical condition of the brain. But what science doesn't uncover is that there is a spiritual aspect of depression as well. This pastor would refer to depression as "navel gazing" because the depressed person is looking down at him or herself instead of looking up to God. When we look down at ourselves so intensely that all we see are the flaws, we overanalyze our feelings without questioning their validity against scripture or thinking about their impact on ourselves and others. It's almost impossible to see the blessings God has given you and the work that God may have for you to do if you are always looking down at the ground.

In Chapter 1 of this book, I shared my story about living with a husband who suffered anxiety and depression. Now it's his turn to share. I asked Mike to help me with this chapter as he also continually works to fight off feelings of depression and anxiety. He found a road to healing when he stopped "navel gazing," and he has done this by changing his perspective and without clinical counseling or medication.

Mike's Story

When I was a kid, I was afraid of what may be lurking in the dark at night. Many children have this common reaction to the dark, and perhaps you have as well. But as I've grown, I've noticed that my response to stressors can easily be one of anxiety.

As Charity has already discussed, I struggled with intense anxiety and depression early in our marriage. In my case, when I allowed my anxiety to spiral, I would experience feelings of depression. Depression seemed to closely follow my anxiety, likely due to the exhausting work of being anxious. You can imagine how unattractive this was to my new wife.

What made it so hard for her was that I was not working to provide for our newly formed family, nor was I able to be a strong emotional support for her. In addition to all that, I was sucking the fun out of the room. I had lost much of my motivation, frequently feeling anxious and sad, and I struggled to feel joy.

I was reluctant to seek clinical counseling, but Charity convinced me to meet with my childhood pastor. After meeting with him a few times, I learned that a major part of my problem was that I was disproportionately focused on myself. Stuck in my anxious thoughts, I trusted very few people. My childhood pastor was one of the few people I actually trusted, so I was able to hear and receive his guidance.

One of the main concepts that helped me in my struggle was to understand what my excessive introspection was doing to my wife. Something I learned from my time with my pastor that made a huge difference was this: *Even if your thoughts are self-deprecating and critical, focusing on yourself at the expense of others is selfish.*

I thought I was doing this commendable thing by thinking so lowly of myself. I thought I was being humble, but really I was being selfish. My pastor called this excessive introspection "navel gazing." Though a humble view of self is important, focusing *only* on oneself, is selfish and is not biblical. But we can also be selfish in a positive or inflated view of ourselves. Regardless of how we think of ourselves, we hurt those around us when we only think of ourselves.

I didn't want to be selfish. I didn't want to hurt my new wife. And I didn't want to suck the fun out of the room. I hadn't thought of my actions as selfish, but that's what they were.

So what is a practical takeaway that I've learned? God wants us to care for others in how we think. Don't allow negative thoughts and sad or anxious feelings to cause you to only think of yourself. Not only will this shift in perspective benefit those around you, but it will also benefit you. When you change your perspective enough to focus on the needs of others, you will begin to lessen the focus on yourself. This can help lessen your anxiety and depression. When we adopt perspectives that better match what God intends for us, there are benefits.

CHAPTER 11

PERSPECTIVE CHANGE IS HEART CHANGE

Though we have been learning about perspective, we must understand that God judges us on our hearts, and He transforms us through our hearts (Genesis 6:5, Romans 12:2). Our perspectives are a matter of our hearts. When we give our heart to the Lord, we receive a new motivation, a new purpose, and a new sense of self. To have a true perspective change, our hearts must change as well. God's primary concern for us is the state of our hearts. This should be our primary objective as well. The Bible tells us that our hearts can either be made of stone or made of flesh (Ezekiel 11:19).

When I was a young adult, there was a situation in which someone I cared for and respected, and who was in authority over me, believed that I was against him. He believed that I was trying to get people to think badly of him. He believed that, because I pierced my nose, I was trying to get unhealthy attention from boys, and because I was advocating for other people whom he had authority over, I was trying to turn people against him. I am unsure of my exact actions at the time as it is all a blur, and it is likely that I did not handle everything perfectly.

When I tried to talk to him about it, and even brought in

christian leadership, I explained that my intention was to be helpful and to try to mediate between him and the others. He did not believe me. I tried to explain that my heart was loving toward him and the others in the group and I was trying to work things out in a godly manner. He told me that "we will have to agree to disagree." I asked, "you mean we are going to agree to disagree about what the nature of my heart is?" and he confirmed that was how he saw it. I responded, "I will not agree to that."

As you can imagine, that was like a knife right through the heart. I can actually still feel the breathless, burning pit in my stomach that his words triggered in me. I walked out of the meeting and burst into tears and walked away from that situation and all of the people that were involved. God has brought healing to me since, but when talking about the heart, I have to say: *Only God knows your heart.*

Our heart is the core of our inner being, and our heart is made up of our feelings, motivations, and insights. It is who we are. It develops our intuition and operates our minds, which constitutes the operation of thinking, reasoning, and forming our logic. Our perspective is directly linked to both our thinking and our hearts. However, for our new perspectives and functions of the mind to stick, heart change is necessary. You can try to change how you think and how you look at things by willing your heart to do something different, but if you want freedom from stress, anxiety, depression, and negative feelings, your heart has to change as well. God knows our heart, judges us on our heart, and is the only one who can change your heart.

The more we choose to deepen our relationship with God, the more heart change we will experience. In Chapter 7 of this book, we talked about following God's commands to keep ourselves healthy in body, soul, mind, and relationships. With a heart awakened and softened by God, we not only concern ourselves with our own health, but also we consider how our hearts and actions bring glory to God.

> Search me, God, and know my heart; test me and know my anxious thoughts. See if there is any offensive way in me, and lead me in the way everlasting.
>
> (Psalm 139:23–24)

Exchange Your Heart

Jesus is the one who exchanges our heart of stone with a new heart, exchanging a heart of unforgiveness, bitterness, selfishness, and discontentment with a heart that is humble, rejoices in the forgiveness of our sins, and treats others the way the Lord has treated us.

One of the most common reasons that people deny faith in Jesus is the sinfulness of other believers and the pride shown by those who proclaim a Christian faith. This is because people can often see the condition of the heart even when attempts are made to conceal it.

Consider how your pride looks to others if you want to pass along the hope of the gospel and a proper perspective to others. Sadly we have all had times where others may have perceived us in that way, especially when we were new in our faith. However, as the Lord works in us, we are to aim at bringing glory to God through our actions, words, behaviors, and attitudes.

> So whether you eat or drink or whatever you do, do it all
> for the glory of God.
>
> (1 Corinthians 10:31)

Sometimes we fail to bring glory to God in the ways that we relate to other people. Some scholars explain that Jesus showed 100% grace and 100% truth when relating to people. Jesus is a perfect being, so He was able to do this gracefully. We are not perfect. When we are still learning how to strive for the 100% truth and the 100% love that is shown to us in Jesus, we often come across as contradictory. The best way to bring glory to God is to humble ourselves and love others. We need to be willing to admit that, although we are learning to better understand the things of God, we are not God. Only God is God, and in our humanity, we are sometimes wrong in our thoughts, actions, and behaviors.

I believe many of the denominational conflicts could be sorted out if we all took a more humble attitude toward biblical interpretation. Most of the time, theological disagreements stem from a pure-hearted place of wanting to better understand God and the Bible. Only we are best served if we consider the views of others with a posture of humility. We often think of humbling ourselves as something we should do, and yet passionate and prideful opinions continue to rise loudly to the top of many topics we chose to discuss such as theology, politics, money, and parenting choices.

I do believe that God humbles us when we do not humble ourselves. Some of the hardships in your life may be opportunities for you to humble yourself before the Lord. Friend, I pray that you will be able to let go of misinterpretations of others motivations, as well as prideful opinions, so that you can increase the effect you can have on others for the glory of God. I pray you are able to humble yourself, and embrace God's provision and sovereignty in your life. I pray that you can trust Him to guide you where you need to go. I pray that you will have a hunger in your heart to make decisions and live your life in a way that brings glory to God.

> Humble yourselves before the Lord, and he will lift you up.
>
> (James 4:10)

Maintaining a Heart of Flesh

Proverbs 4:20–27 tells us to guard our heart. You have probably heard that before but there is more to be discovered in the passage where we find that command.

> My son, pay attention to what I say; turn your ear to my words. Do not let them out of your sight, keep them within your heart; for they are life to those who find them and health to one's whole body. Above all else, guard your heart, for everything you do flows from it. Keep your mouth free of perversity; keep corrupt talk far from your lips. Let your eyes look straight ahead; fix your gaze directly before you. Give careful thought to the paths for your feet and be steadfast in all your ways. Do not turn to the right or the left; keep your foot from evil.
>
> (Proverbs 4:20–27)

We are to be attentive to His words and incline our ears to His sayings. The passage tells us to keep His Word in our heart and guard our heart because from our heart flows everything we do.

This passage is what this book has been about.

To experience this heart change we have to understand God's truth, and we have to have a proper perspective using God's truth as our lens (Proverbs 4:20–22). We have to have a proper perspective about God, ourselves, our enemy, our fear, our feelings, and our relationships—all of it. When you are going through a heart change journey, you will look back and realize that you have indeed been growing. You will be farther along in your sanctification journey than you were before, and you will be able to live out God's plans for your life more fully.

- What heart changes are you sensing in your life today?
- What perspective, attitude, or heart change has God been leading you toward?
- What are you going to do to embrace this change?
- How can you practically change your habits to ensure that you remember this heart change you are experiencing?

Guard Your Heart

In Proverbs 4:23, it states "Above all else, guard your heart...." This makes one thing very clear: the state of your heart is the most important thing. As a young person I used to think that just meant to protect yourself by not putting yourself in situations in which you would be hurt, but I have grown to understand that the meaning is so much deeper than that. In John 7:38 the Bible tells us that when someone turns to follow Jesus, "rivers of living water will flow from within them." God gives us a heart with new understanding of our meaning, value, and purpose. The heart of stone is full of sinful desires, sinful thinking, and sinful motivations. When Jesus softens our heart and gives us a new heart, our new understanding and perspective gives us the ability to love others, to think selfless-ly, and to see conviction of our sins. Satan and the sinful culture we are all living in try to take away that understanding. We must guard our hearts in order to not lose that new understanding and perspective on the meaning and purpose of life.

We are to guard our hearts so that our hearts do not become filled with anger, ungratefulness, and pride. We are to protect our-selves in spiritual warfare so that we can continue to embrace our newfound meaning and purpose and be convicted of sinful pat-terns when they inevitably creep into our hearts.

The Bible gives examples of those who have hardened their hearts. In Exodus 7 and 8, Pharaoh's hard heart, full of sin, caused him to ignore the miraculous works of God and stand against God's people. The sinfulness in his heart left him in a place to re-main an enemy of God's kingdom. Sin that you allow to remain in your heart may cause you to ignore the work of God in your life.

Our Heart's Effect on Others

Our heart is the instrument with which we connect with other people. We can affect others' hearts by the state of our own heart (Proverbs 23:18, Proverbs 27:9, Proverbs 15:13). We are called to do two things as children of God. One is to grow in our knowledge of and relationship with God, and the other is to share the gospel with others. This can be summed up with the following:

> "Teacher, which is the greatest commandment in the Law?" Jesus replied: "'Love the Lord your God with all your heart and with all your soul and with all your mind.' This is the first and greatest commandment. And the sec-

ond is like it: 'Love your neighbor as yourself.' All the Law
and the Prophets hang on these two commandments."

(Matthew 22:36–40)

As you grow deeper in your relationship with the Lord, you
will learn to love Him with all your soul and all your mind and all
your heart. Your perspective will be transforming one lesson at a
time which will soften your heart. Strive to get yourself in a place
in which you have a good and healthy heart so that you can then
pass along that goodness to others. Your perspective and your attitude toward life, the world, others, and God will be contagious
to your family, your friends, and your coworkers. Make sure that
your heart is in a good place so that you can pass along a positive
perspective and not a negative one.

As you are learning to love the Lord with all your heart and all
your mind, you will be passing along the wisdom you are gaining.
You will pass along a piece of the perspective that you are embracing as others hear the joy and excitement that comes from your
deeper relationship with the Lord.

We all affect other people more than we know. We pass along
our attitudes to others even when we are not attempting to do so.
Keep in mind that what comes out of your mouth flows from your
heart and also affects other people's hearts (Proverbs 4:24).

When I don't get my way, or when I perceive that someone
is taking advantage of me, I am tempted to complain. And when
that happens, I can tell that other people around me also start to
grumble. For me, I know I can be in a fine mood, but then someone starts to complain and my mood changes too. The Bible warns
us against grumbling and gossiping. We affect the people around

us with our words, our attitudes, and the state of our hearts. Even though I still struggle with these things, over the years I've improved. I grumble less and refrain from gossiping as much as possible. Still, while I'm certainly not an expert at refraining from complaining (you can ask my husband), I have learned to better avoid these tempting habits.

It is best to consider our effect on others and attempt to be a positive influence instead of a negative one. I have found that I grow the most when I am supporting others in an area because I can listen to my own words and they remind my heart of the truth. Sometimes the best way to hold onto a proper perspective and cherish the amazing change that God has made in your heart is to pass along a proper perspective to others. Find others whom you can help with their perspective.

- How can you encourage others in their relationship with God?
- How can you pass along a biblical perspective in other people's situations? No one needs anything more than a biblical perspective when they are struggling with life.
- In your relationships with others, are you fueling negative perspectives or encouraging positive perspectives?

Fix Your Eyes on Jesus

Fixing your eyes on the things above will bring about heart change but this takes intention on your part. The more your focus is on an eternal perspective, the more that God's truth sinks deeper into your soul. The more you experience life through an eternal perspective, the richer your experience of healing and peace will be. Intentionally set up habits that will keep your eyes on Christ.

When I can keep my eyes fixed on the things above, and when I refresh my memory on the proper perspectives of things, I am more successful and much less likely to grumble, complain, and pass along a negative perspective (Proverbs 4:25–27). I have noticed that if I go more than 2 or 3 days without intentionally fixing my eyes on God and the purpose He has given my life, then I get selfish, easily annoyed, and start to think negatively. My relationships start to struggle, and I start to feel a bit down and anxious. So you may be asking yourself: How do I fix my eyes on the Lord? Here are my suggestions:

Spend time with God daily. Your mind is a battleground. If God's truth is not renewing your mind daily, then Satan will try to take it over. Just as you have to clean your physical body, consider cleaning your mind with Scripture so that your perspective will flourish rather than becoming unhealthy and skewed.

Avoid negative inputs such as negative movies or media. We are bombarded constantly with worldly input from social media, advertisements, interactions with other people, music, and TV.

Serve others. You need to be in touch with the realities of this world by serving the homeless or comforting the broken hearted. Then you will deepen your Christ-given compassion for the world and remember the joy that comes from freedom in Christ. We can feel the joy of freedom, like a baby learning to walk, if we can keep our eyes on Christ and keep our perspectives straight.

Journal. Take notes or journal about what God is doing in your life and what you are learning. This will help you better apply biblical truth to your everyday life.

Share with others. Tell your friends, or strangers, stories about the lessons God is teaching you and the blessings that God has given you. Consider asking your friends what growth they have seen in you. When you talk about these things, you will have more accountability, and the people in your life can help you remember what you learned and the perspectives that God has given you.

Take pictures. Use them as reminders of the lessons that you are learning, and the many blessings of God in your life.

Don't Forget

If you are like me, it is easy to forget the lessons that you have learned. There are so many details that go into my brain all the time, and things seem to easily slip out the back of my brain. I am also triggered by different things that lead me to battling issues I've already fought. Sometimes I don't realize it is a lesson I've previously learned until I'm already in the middle of the battle again.

For me, it might be an issue with trusting God with finances or a hardship at our business that triggers anxiety and feelings of desperation. Or it might be a messy house or grumpy kids that trigger feelings of failure as a mother. Having a reminder of what God has given me and the perspectives that He has helped me to overcome helps me to straighten out my thoughts when new battles arise. With this perspective, I work through the negative feelings faster, and I am faster to remember to trust the Lord. It is this shift in mindset that helps the burden to lift from my shoulders.

When I forget the perspective I embraced previously, even the same scenario that once taught me to trust God can lead me to have to process the entire lesson all over again. Once I learn a certain lesson or embrace a certain perspective, I try to write it down. If I can remember to read back through it next time something similar arises, I can quickly remember the perspective that was my life raft when I was drowning in stress, anxiety, and negativity.

I have also given myself other reminders such as putting Bible verse decals on the walls of my home and my office, singing Christian songs to my kids at night, and setting passwords to something that reminds me of biblical truth. When I recommitted my life to Christ after Josh died when I was in college, I actually decided to pierce my nose as a reminder of my freedom in Christ and my devotion to live like a new person. I found a verse in Isaiah that mentions God giving Israel jewels to express His love for His people once they returned to Him. So for fifteen years, every time I looked in the mirror and saw my nose piercing I remembered my commitment to no longer compromise my faith. It served as a reminder to live like a new person. With every step I took, I intentionally looked first to God when making decisions.

- How can you remember the lessons God is teaching you?
- How much different will your life be if you remain fully committed to living your life for Christ?
- How might things be different if you continually remember your new found freedom as you embrace a biblical perspective in the different areas of your life?

Friend, remember you are going to forget—just like me. You are going to need reminders and support. If you are struggling with any of the things in this book, I want to encourage you to find a Christian friend, pastor, or Christian counselor who can help you as you work through your challenges. Over the years I have seen different Christian counselors and pastors as I have fought my flesh to embrace these truths—there is no shame in that.

CHAPTER 12

PERSPECTIVE ALLOWS YOU TO EXPERIENCE JOY

When my youngest son was learning to walk, he was so excited and exhilarated to be free of crawling that he giggled and laughed his way through every step. It even took him longer to maintain his balance because he was so tickled that he finally could do what everyone else could do. He finally had freedom. He would take a few steps and just giggle and giggle. He would get to giggling so much that he would lose his balance and fall down. He has always been a happy kid.

After a while, as the walking became more natural to him, he stopped giggling. Once he was fully walking and no longer crawling, it was like he didn't think of it as fun anymore. Walking was just his new normal. As he pushed his limits and tried to focus on running or gaining a new skill, he would show some joy, but shortly after that, the exhilarated giggling stopped. As I watched him, I was kind of sad that walking and running was no longer full of joy and excitement for him, but it made me think about my relationship with Jesus.

So many times when I learn something new or when Jesus sets me free from a negative pattern or a skewed perspective, I experience a sense of freedom. I get really excited and my heart feels full. I tell people around me, and I feel the joy that the freedom of the Holy Spirit brings. But after a little while, as the lesson I learned becomes more a part of my natural rhythms, the joy and excitement starts to fade. It starts to feel more like that's how I deserve to be—free.

I am sometimes hard on myself or mad at myself because I do not understand why I don't feel that joy and passion anymore. It's like I have adjusted to this newfound freedom instead of looking through the lens of what it was like before I experienced the freedom. The excitement gets lost in an expectation that life should just be this way.

But just as my son continues to grow and learn new skills of running, climbing, and jumping, we are to continue to grow in our relationship with Jesus. As I continue to grow deeper in my relationship with the Lord through life's trials, I am starting to understand the Bible verse in James:

> Consider it pure joy, my brothers and sisters, whenever you face trials of many kinds, because you know that the testing of your faith produces perseverance. Let perseverance finish its work so that you may be mature and complete, not lacking anything.
>
> (James 1:2–4)

Finding Joy

Joy comes from an understanding of, and an awe for, our Holy Creator, while remembering that we are still sinners saved by grace. We do not deserve the gift Jesus gave us, but it was given to us because of His abundant love for us. Sometimes we are so used to our new-found identity in Christ that it's easy to forget who we were without Him. Without Christ we were just sinners born into a sinful world and held captive to sin; we actually deserve to experience pain, sadness, sickness, and eventually death. We do still live in this sinful world, and we do still have a sin nature that we must die to daily. There are consequences for the sins that we continue with, and we will continue to struggle with sin until we're with Jesus. However, the joy of our redemption can override those challenges.

To find joy in our redemption, we need to remember to count our blessings and focus on the positives. We need to remember how good God has been to us and be thankful for God's provision, His sacrifice, and His plan for our lives. If we can keep the perspective that we are depraved and surrender to Jesus' lordship in our lives, and if we can remain thankful for all of the good things that God has given us, I believe we'll be able to experience joy and hold onto the passion and energy we have for Christ much longer.

I learned about the importance of finding joy and how forgetting our blessings can hide joy through a situation at my work. Being a business owner I usually hear about every problem that needs fixed, and it's rare to receive encouragement when things are going well. When you are a leader, people often misjudge your actions and look at the negative things as personal statements about how you feel about them.

In building our business, we have had many ups and downs, and we have had to focus on certain areas of the business during specific seasons in order to grow. During one such season, our focus was pulled away from our staff as we fixed other underlying problems with the operation of the business. During that time we experienced an influx in staff complaints. It felt like any time we would fix something that one person complained about, another person would complain about what we fixed. Soon after, a new complaint would arise and the pattern repeated itself.

When we first hire new staff, they are often excited to be working with us. We do care about our staff, and we put effort toward making our business a nice place to work. After a while though, the excitement wears off, and sometimes a few of those working with us start to feel like maybe there should be something else to make it better. As this became a recurrence, I took it to prayer.

I was feeling taken advantage of and unappreciated, and it made me want to hide from people. Some of the complaints were personal and based on misunderstandings. It was hard to stand strong against the criticism because I knew the sacrifices that we were making to keep the business running. I was growing bitter because we often did try really hard to keep our staff happy. I was feeling offended that staff kept complaining about little things and assuming that we could not be trusted. Then God convicted me.

In prayer, God made it clear to me. I am no different in my perspective at times. I am prone to the same human pattern in my relationship with Him. I had no place being bitter about others losing their perspective. I forget to count my blessings. I allow the stressors of life to influence my attitude. I focus on how things could be better for me rather than focusing on how good I have it. I question if God can be trusted when things don't work out in my favor. I forget to be thankful for His sacrifice. It is so easy to do, and we all do it. Since then, we have been able to make some structural changes in our business which have minimized the complaints.

Instead of staying offended and wanting to hide, I am now able to take my business relationships to Jesus. In doing so, I am humbled because I often find myself guilty of the same human pattern of a negative attitude. It helps me to be strengthened by Jesus during the times when Satan tells me I should just quit and stop trying to be nice to people.

A negative attitude is so easy to fall into. A negative attitude will prohibit you from finding joy in your life.

- Do you count your blessings?
- Do you practice an attitude of contentment, or do you always wonder what could be better?
- Are you able to have a thankful heart knowing God is taking care of you?
- Can you have patience knowing that God has a plan for your life and He knows exactly what you are enduring?
- Can you consider it pure joy to endure hardships as Christ did, knowing that it will build perseverance and faith?

Embracing Joy

A conclusion to the life lessons I've learned from God so far comes down to Joy. For my whole life I was sceptical that I would ever really experience Joy because I was too anxious minded and task-driven. Friend, I have learned how to experience Joy, and I am a completely different person because of it. I have learned that experiencing Joy takes significant effort on my part. It means having a proper perspective rooted in God's truth. It means taking my thoughts captive and submitting them to the truth. It means fighting my sinful flesh, my will, and my negative thoughts. It means standing up to Satan and not allowing him to manipulate my perspective. I have to spend time with God, deepening my relationship with Him regularly, to continue feeling the Joy of new freedoms every day. I have to embrace a perspective of Joy in the Lord.

Embracing this perspective of Joy in the Lord involves choosing to define God and myself as the Bible does. It means surrendering my plans for my life to God's will and viewing my trials as worthy conduits in furthering God's kingdom. I have to be willing to give up control. I have to be willing to embrace my piece in the puzzle. It means being willing to play my role with confidence that our Holy Creator knows what is best for me. It means knowing that the highs and lows in my life have potential to bring glory to Him and win souls for the Kingdom of Christ.

Joy in the Lord will not come if I don't intentionally submit my thought life to the truth of the Bible and if I do not choose to release feelings of fear and stress to the Lord. It means stepping out in faith in relationships with other people and surrendering my own ideas and ways of thinking for biblical truth. I have to practice what I have learned. I have to choose to overcome depressive feelings and temptations to only consider myself. I have to choose not to fear the unknown, choose not to be anxious for tomorrow, and choose not to be moody and judgmental because things didn't go my way.

I have to confront Satan and the lies that have turned into strongholds in my life. I have to keep my eyes fixed on the Lord Jesus and place my trust in His plans no matter what events I encounter in my life. I have to remember that this world is not my home and living for eternity is the purpose of my life on earth. I have to surrender the care of those I love to the Lord. I have to still my heart and live one moment at a time embraced by the arms of my Savior. I have to remember these perspectives and practice them at every turn, even if a new trial or time of suffering presents itself.

Practicing Joy

Just as I was about to turn in this book for final editing God gave me a chance to practice what I have been writing about. I went to a doctor's appointment and they found a spot on my skin that was suspicious. The doctor said, "Well it is hard to tell if it is just a mole or if it is cancerous; we probably should shave it off and biopsy it." I agreed and scheduled to come back in two weeks. I felt okay remembering that I am living my life for Jesus, and if it is in His plan for me to battle cancer, then I will willingly do it. I committed to intentionally learning every lesson I can through whatever path God has for me.

However, as I got in the car and started driving home I sensed Satan trying to attack me with all the fiery darts that he threw at me during my third pregnancy. I had intrusive thoughts about the pain and fear my kids might endure, and thoughts about the physical pain I may have to go through. I began to feel fear of losing my spunk, my energy, and my ability to be an involved mom if I had to go through cancer treatments. I stopped myself there and fought off the intrusive thoughts, but I could feel my emotions still rising. When I stopped at a stop light, I felt I needed to imagine Jesus sitting right next to me. I began to imagine what He might say to me. I imagined Jesus looking into my eyes while saying that He was with me. I imagined Him holding my hand and saying He knew the plan He had for me. This helped the truth of the Bible better connect with my emotions.

When I got home, I sat in the driveway for a while. I told God that I would go wherever He leads because I trust Him and I believe that His will for my life will bring the most progress for His Kingdom. I told Him that I know He loves my kids more than I do, and I surrendered their lives to Him. I told Him I trusted that He would turn all things to good according to His purpose. I said this out loud, not for God's sake but rather for my own. Declaring my stance helped me to submit my anxiety and my fleshly desire to have control. In doing so, I was able to choose joy in the Lord.

I also got angry at Satan, and I declared to him "you have no power over my thoughts. I will not be afraid. I will not allow you to take my peace and joy. Flee from me in the name of Jesus." I then focused my thoughts back onto Jesus and what good He has for me regardless of the path. It then occurred to me that my editor wanted me to add a conclusion to my book that would offer readers something to better hold onto. Then it hit me, this is a chance to practice what I have been writing about. At that moment, I realized that through the trial of waiting on results and possibly receiving a cancer diagnosis, I was given the opportunity to deepen my trust in God. For the first time in my life, the invitation of James 1:2–4—considering it joy to go through a trial—felt very much within my reach.

My emotions were starting to settle, but there was one more thing that I needed to grasp in order to feel God's peace again. In my head, I knew all the things I had written about trusting God, but for some reason my emotions still felt intensely high. As I talked with my husband Mike, my kids walked into the room and I began to tear up. I prayed and tried to process my emotions. Then I realized, I was not afraid of this skin spot. I believe that if it was cancerous God would give me the strength to persevere, I would fight it, and God's will would prevail bringing Him the most glory no matter the outcome.

As I fought off the intrusive thoughts of fear, I realized the tearful emotions were stemming from my past fear that I endured during my third pregnancy when I was faced with a seemingly life or death decision. My tears were a trauma response. It was a new layer to the trauma that I still needed to grieve and process in order to embrace God's peace and joy in this situation.

I continued to process my feelings, and more layers emerged. I remembered feeling so alone during that pregnancy as I feared for my kids and the potential of them growing up without a mama. I processed how this new situation really wasn't that scary. I did not really feel worried, but my emotions were still heavy. I went through half a box of tissues processing this new dark corner of that past trauma, and then I realized I was also behind on sleep. The combination of post-trauma and lack of sleep was fueling my emotional reaction. Eventually I allowed myself a nap, and when I woke up, I experienced immense peace.

I was able to feel the confidence, peace, and joy that I have been writing about. If I had not analyzed why I was feeling the way I was, and if I had not fought off the attacks from Satan, I would have been sucked back into fear, anxiety, and worry. I would have wondered how I lost all the growth I had gained over the past few years. As a therapist, it was exciting to experience the great impact that comes with analyzing feelings and their roots. It made me even more honored and joyful that God has called me to be a therapist and author because I get to help others find this freedom from their emotions too.

My friend, I had to make a choice to identify where my emotions were coming from, fight my sinful desire to make my own plan for every variable, and reject Satan's lies in order to not allow fear, worry, and emotions to steal my peace and joy. I had to intentionally search for hidden strongholds, dark corners of pain, and improper perspectives so that I did not lose my joy, confidence, and peace during the trial.

As I waited to get results from my biopsy, I still encountered a few fearful and anxious thoughts at times, but I continued practicing taking those thoughts captive and making them submissive to an eternal perspective. Sometimes I would think, "Hopefully if it's cancerous I don't have to take any medicine and feel terrible all the time. How can I be a good mom if I feel sick." I then reminded myself that God is my strength. He gives me strength to get through any trial. When I would think, "Maybe I should research and find out how my life will change if this is cancer," I then told myself, "No, I don't need to know right now. I will take it as it comes and deal with it then." I have continued to mentally recite the following verse in Matthew:

> Therefore do not worry about tomorrow, for tomorrow will worry about itself. Each day has enough trouble of its own.
>
> (Matthew 6:34)

Practicing an eternal perspective and putting my trust in God for every step I take allowed me to keep joy and peace in my heart even in the time of waiting, something that I have never been able to experience before. I would still wake up before my children and worship the Lord for all He has done in my life, instead of waking up scared, anxious, and stressed. I visited my therapist during this time to help me verbally process and explain what thoughts were trying to creep into my heart and steal my peace. She brought to my attention how anxious I used to be and how I am a whole new person now, transformed by the renewing of my mind. By washing my mind with biblical truth and embracing a biblical perspective as I worked through the pages of this book, I experienced redemption and healing at a deeper level than I ever imagined. She reminded me that I literally had diagnosable clinical anxiety at times in my life, even taking medications after traumas in the past. For those two weeks I waited patiently without worry or anxiety until I finally received my results that showed the skin spot was benign.

Today, I have peace and joy and a strength to face trials and suffering. I am able to keep negative thoughts and feelings in submission to Christ and not be consumed with fear. I know that my earthly life is dispensable, and it will come to an end, but my eternal life is invaluable and secure. I can let go of the feeling I have to control my life, anxiously protect my children, and make all the right choices in attempts to avoid hardship. Keeping my eyes fixed on God's purposes has allowed me to embrace the eternal purpose of living my life every day to bring glory to God. I am delighted that I am able to live out God's highest purpose for my life. I have learned the power in knowing that my life is not meant to escape trials, suffering, and persecution, but rather my life has a greater purpose. I can face hardship with a Christlie joy and confidence because of my Heavenly Father's will for my life.

- My friend, what are you facing today?
- What hardship, trial, or suffering are you trying to avoid?

- What stress are you facing?
- What doubt, attacks from Satan, or self-destructive thinking are you struggling with?
- What sinful anger, hidden strongholds, selfish attitudes, fleshly desires, or skewed perspectives are you battling?

I want to encourage you to live today with peace and joy knowing that Jesus will give you the strength to endure, persevere, and triumph over each trial in your life. Pay attention to the conviction and guidance of the Holy Spirit, and allow Him to comfort you and lead you into Christlike thinking. Let God have control over your life, your thinking, your feelings, and your circumstances. Be still and know that He is God, and that you are loved and valuable. He will take care of you and your loved ones. Rest in Him and surrender your fear, anxieties, and stress to Him. His yoke is easy and His burden is light. (Psalm 46:10, 1 Peter 4:11, Matthew 11:30).

Writing this book, reviewing the lessons God has taught me, editing them over and over, and intentionally connecting Scripture to them, has changed my life.

Perspective is the first major hurdle for a deepening relationship with God. The next is intentionally applying it to your life and in your trials. My greatest passion as a Christian counselor and author is helping my clients and my audience to deepen their relationship with God, embrace their worth in Christ, and release their anxieties to the Lord so that they can rest in His peace and joy. My deepest prayer for you is that you will be filled with the confidence to walk out His eternal calling on your life.

Friend, thank you for sharing this journey with me. I pray God blesses you with abundance as you apply these lessons to your life.

EPILOGUE

THE PANDEMIC

This book was not going to have an epilogue. I was finished. I had moved my focus to my children's books and started research for my next book. But shortly after I turned in this manuscript for final edits, the coronavirus pandemic hit. I woke up one morning and knew I had to add one more perspective before submitting this book for printing.

The same week that I was finishing up the last edit with my talented editor, our governor closed all schools. Soon after that, gatherings of large crowds were banned. Then restaurant dining rooms closed, then incidental activities and then non-essential businesses. Finally, people were ordered by the government to stay in their homes for an unknown length of time. Seemingly overnight, we had to shut down our office location, and our business faced a whirlwind of details to work out in order to allow our therapists to still provide treatment to our clients remotely. No matter what, our business would take a hit, and our clients would have to make adjustments. If you are reading this many years after the publishing date, it's Spring 2020. The coronavirus is quickly spreading and everyone is bracing themselves to survive the pandemic.

Many people are highly anxious, the media seems to be convincing people that everyone will get the virus and some may die suddenly. Fear is in the air. As I look around me, I realize that, had God not allowed me the blessing of writing this book over the last year, I would not have developed the lessons He taught me through the writing, reading, and editing of these words and the scriptures that support the content. Without the journey of this book, I too would be strung out on anxious thoughts during this tragic time of global pandemic.

As Mike and I rearranged our lives to follow orders and continue to manage three kids, a business, book publishing, and a new puppy (we decided to get the puppy long before the threat of the virus), we were experiencing some stress. But I didn't feel anxious and fearful like I used to feel. I wasn't worried about money, although our business stood to lose half of our income. Money isn't an idol for me anymore. God has broken the stronghold of finances in my life. I was unshaken, yet only a few years ago I would have experienced emotional breakdowns when faced with skipping a paycheck, lost income, or accruing debt. Today I am a new person. I can dance to worship music while writing this, knowing that God will take care of my family and me, and I have faith that His plans are greater than my plans—both personally and professionally.

The virus keeps multiplying, and while we are still wiping down our groceries with bleach wipes as recommended, I am not afraid of getting sick. I do not have thoughts of what if someone in my family dies or what if I die, even though the media would like for me to think otherwise (we have stopped watching the news, by the way.) Those thoughts were a strong part of my brain's thought patterns for so many years, even as recently as two years ago during my last pregnancy. However, now they are like a feather in the wind. I notice anxious thoughts for a quick moment but then they are gone.

I feel so blessed that I am able to remember that this world is NOT my home. I remind myself that I am here for a purpose. When that purpose is over I will get to go home to be with Jesus. I am here on assignment with a mission to bring God's glory to this world, and my heavenly Father is in control.

Jesus Take Control

Being able to release the feeling of responsibility and the temptation to be in control of this situation—a situation that is in no way controllable—has allowed me to have peace during chaos. I am experiencing chaos both inside my home and certainly outside my home.

Everything is unknown. How long will this last? How many people will get the virus? How many people will die? What will the economy be like after this? Will my children get to go back to school this year or even the next school year? Will my children get to grow up in the America I knew as a child or will all the depictions of cultural devastation from the movies become a reality after this? With almost everything unknown and with growing fear of sickness, increased demands on those with essential jobs, and a completely different routine for children and those with non-essential jobs, the whole world is now fully aware that we do not have the power to control anything. Many of us are realizing that we need to turn to the One who is in control.

I have been talking to people about their stories as they transition to a new normal during this time of quarantine. Many people have awesome stories of what God has done in their lives over the last few months that is now allowing them to experience blessing as they are home with their families around the clock. What I have heard over and over is this: The legs have been removed from their idols of financial security, control, vanity, other's opinions, and busyness, and now people are seeing their need for God more clearly than ever before. As a result, more people are able to be present with their families during these uncertain times.

I have heard time and time again that Christians are praying more than ever. Maybe they are doing so out of fear, loneliness, or compassion, but no matter the reason, they are praying. God is using this to turn people to Himself.

It is such a blessing to have a perspective that looks for God's plans in every situation. It is such a blessing to have grown into a person who now remains calm when chaos ensues. I now rest in the assurance that God, who loves us more than we can imagine, is in control of everything. I am energized by watching God put the pieces together as He brings glory to Himself in this time of catastrophe.

I am not claiming that I don't get overwhelmed with it all. Trying to multitask basically every minute of the day is stressful. I am tired. My brain feels like it is mush. But, I am not afraid and anxious like I have been in the past. I am not ruled by my emotions because I have found peace and joy by embracing a Christ-centered, biblical, and eternal perspective.

Friend, if you are struggling to embrace a Christ-centered, biblical, and eternal perspective, whether it is during the time of the pandemic or another time in your life long after the 2020 coronavirus pandemic is over, I want to encourage you to spend time in God's Word and prayer. Use this time to introduce more quietness with God than you have allowed in your life before. Get to know Him closer, and grow in your trust of Him. Surrender your fears and give Jesus control over your emotions and your life.

An illustration I use with my clients is this: Think of a person in your life that you know and trust. Name that person. What if they told you they wanted to take you somewhere—just the two of you—but they couldn't tell you where you were going. They told you that they knew every step of the way and would take care of everything. They then told you the trip might be uncomfortable or a little painful, but they would take care of you. They assured you that in the end, it would be good for you. Would you be willing to go with them? Would you relax and stop worrying about all the details of what was going to happen next, trusting that they are dependable and would take care of you like they promised?

Typically people say yes they would still go, though not all people say yes. I ask those who say yes, why? Why say yes knowing that almost all aspects of the situation will be out of their control. People typically answer that they would say yes because they know the person and they trust that person wouldn't put them in harm's way. They trust that person wouldn't make them do something that they hated doing. They are confident of all of this because they KNOW them.

Friend, how well do you KNOW Jesus? When you know Him, you can hand over control of your life and surrender your anxiety and fear. You can live knowing that even if the journey is uncomfortable or painful, you can trust that wherever Jesus takes you, it will all work together for your good (Romans 8:28).

Surrendering Frustration and Grief

Even though I do not feel afraid of the virus, of course there are a few fearful thoughts that I have to take captive and submit to Christ. I still get a bit teary or frustrated as every day feels the same and I grieve the loss of self care activities I enjoyed only a few weeks ago. I miss going to the gym and I miss date night. I miss the stillness of sitting in a silent house to focus on writing about my journey with the Lord. Sometimes I get sad and mad when I feel the loss.

When I feel frustrated about what is happening and Mike and I are stuck working from home while homeschooling our kids without reinforcements such as school, babysitters, and grandparents, I have to refocus my thoughts. I reframe the situation, remembering that my house is not some place where I am stuck and cannot get out, but rather that my home is a place of safety that will help improve the chances of lowering the spread of the virus. It helps when I remind myself to think of others rather than solely focusing on myself.

I also have to remember to consider what God's eternal purpose is for allowing this pandemic to occur. It helps me to consider what good He may be bringing to my life through this time of trial and extra pressure. God, being consistent in character, is likely using this to turn people to Himself and to help Christians remember His place of importance in their lives. He is the only One who can bring security to our lives, and though it may be a while before we get through this, we can trust that it will be worth it.

I know how stubborn I have been. I know how long it has taken me to have a heart change and really surrender my life fully to God and His plans. It is possible that it may take a while for Him to reach certain people. It may be that the longer that this lasts, the more souls will ultimately turn to the Lord. Maybe the more lonely, nervous, overwhelmed, and bored we feel, the more we will turn to prayer and Scripture to find peace. The frustration subsides when I think of this time in these ways. The more time this pandemic continues, possibly the bigger the impact God can make in people's lives.

There will likely continue to be some moments I tear up because of the feelings of loss—a loss of balance, a loss of healthy activities, and the distance of relationships. Grief is natural and we are all going through it. Some have had to postpone their weddings, cancel graduation ceremonies, or celebrate their birthdays without their friends. Grandparents miss the hugs of their grandbabies, moms miss their alone time, teachers miss getting to watch their students learn, parents miss their date nights, kids miss their friends, essential workers miss the feeling of being safe at work, and sadly, some are grieving the loss of loved ones who have died from this virus. The world is grieving. Allow yourself to mourn your losses. Allow yourself to grieve but do not remain stuck there; allow the Holy Spirit to comfort you.

Matthew 5 has some comforting words for us.

"Blessed are the poor in spirit, for theirs is the kingdom of heaven. Blessed are those who mourn, for they will be comforted. Blessed are the meek, for they will inherit the earth. Blessed are those who hunger and thirst for righteousness, for they will be filled.

(Matthew 5:3-6)

Be humble and look for God's good work through this time in your life, keeping your hope in the promise of eternity with Jesus. Allow the Holy Spirit to comfort you in your grief as you look to eternal purpose in all things. Be gentle and loving with those around you, showing the love of Jesus. Thirst for more of God in your life and seek Him. Commit to living in righteousness. Focusing on these things will allow you to embrace peace and joy even in times of difficulty such as a global pandemic.

Friend, you are in my prayers as you weather this storm and embrace the impact of this catastrophic point in time. Writing this today, it is still very uncertain how it may change our definition of normal life. But I hope you can find comfort in knowing that God is in control.

> And we know that in all things God works for the good of those who love him, who have been called according to his purpose.
>
> (Romans 8:28)

I will be renewing my mind with that verse as we all endure the rollercoaster loops in this unknown season of life. I encourage you to do the same.

Blessing,
Charity

Made in United States
North Haven, CT
06 August 2023

40002650R00125